"UNORTHODOX - CONTROVERSIAL - UNCONVENTIONAL"

POETRY LYRICS

By
The Australian Unauthordox Poet
Garry William Gosney

GARRY GOSNEY

© 1999, to current date Garry William Gosney

ALL RIGHTS RESERVED
No part of this book may be reproduced, stored in a retrieval system, or transmitted by any means, electronic, mechanical,
photocopying, recording, or otherwise, without written permission from the author.

"UNORTHODOX - CONTROVERSIAL - UNCONVENTIONAL"

To Someone ever so Special

Your special for you are my friend

You're the beauty in my life

For without you my friend I am nothing

God bless you my friend

May our friendship continue to prosper

For the true beauty is having you for my friend

Ti Amo forever more

GARRY GOSNEY

My Dedication

UNORTHODOX CONTROVERSIAL UNCONVENTIONAL POETRY LYRICS

To my children Bradley & Grand-daughter Courtney Sky & Michael & Aaron & Daniel & Grand-daughter Kelsie & Grand-son Lucas and Valerie Jean & Grandson -Triston

Even though we are worlds and thousands of miles apart You will always be in my heart and my prayers and you have my love

To all my friends who told me to publish these Without their encouragement none of this would have been possible

For they are special

Without them it would have been impossible as they are Some of my biggest inspiration But the one that deserves the credit is GOD Without his help none of this would ever be possible And I thank the publishers for taking me on I hope you all like and that the words come out all right Please feel free to email me anytime with you comments

"UNORTHODOX - CONTROVERSIAL - UNCONVENTIONAL"

garrygosney@yahoo.com

© 1999, to current date Garry William Gosney

Table of Contents

My Dedication iv

Other Books by the Author 1

Winter Storms and Firelight 2

The Storytellers 5

Realestate Agents and Landlords 6

Is It Reincarnation Or Destiny 8

What Do You See in Me 11

Take Me Back 12

End of an Era, End of A Legend 13

Lest We Forget 9/11 2001 15

Unorthodox Controversial Unconventional 17

Friendship... What is Friendship? 18

Stop The World 20

Things I Miss the Most 21

Happy Trails 22

The Old Oak Tree 24

Merry Christmas Everyone 25

Living a Dream Playing Out a Nightmare 27

Australia My Heart Australia My Home 29

"UNORTHODOX - CONTROVERSIAL - UNCONVENTIONAL"

Yesterday Dreams - Todays Fantasy - Tomorrows Reality 30

Still Playing Let's Pretend 31

April 16th massacre 2007 32

0.3842 Cents A Life 34

The Colours of Change the Colours of Joy 36

Oh Snow Beautiful Snow Lovely Winter Snow 37

Six Years on And More to Come 38

Things Life Taught Us 39

Sing Sing 40

El Dorado El Dorado My El Dorado 41

Pass It on to All Mankind 42

Traditional Christmas 43

Northern Lights of Christmas 45

Christmas in The Bush 47

Christmas Memories 48

Santa is Here 50

My Man 51

Just What Are Memories Made Of 53

Australian Summer 55

Snowbirds Singing 56

Living Stories	57
A Shearer's Life	58
I Wonder Why Maybe So	59
Nature At Its Best	61
Music is the Universal Language	62
There's A Song Deep Within My Heart	63
Spirit of the Mountain	64
When Your Heart Has Left the Building	65
Kentucky Road	68
I Wish I Could Fly	69
Please Forgive Me	70
3 Day September 08 Boycott	72
Shared Along the Way	74
A Mother's Prayer	75
A Fathers Love	76
The Question Is Better Asked	78
Oh What A Majestic Sight to See	81
Live Your Dream	83
A Woman In The Making	85
My MOM	87

"UNORTHODOX - CONTROVERSIAL - UNCONVENTIONAL"

Picture They Call Life 89

Seven Years of Living Memories 91

The Legacy of the Flag 93

The Year Is 2008 The Month Is October 95

The Recession Of Greed 97

Homesick 99

The Beauty of a Recession 100

A Pathetic Place to Live 102

God Bless The World 105

Times Have Changed the World 107

The World Has Spoken 110

Christmas Recession 2008 113

Questioning Incompetence 115

Things We Are Not Suppose To KNOW 117

Just What Are We Looking For 120

17th November The Day I Died 121

The Rules of Choice 123

He Cries Not for Himself 125

Every Reason Escapes ME 127

Let My Heart Whisper 128

Many Faces of Christmas.. 129

Small Town Christmas.. 131

Do You Believe.. 132

Fake Promises and Broken Truths 134

Real-Estate Agents in the Mid-West Geraldton 136

They Deserve Life Death by Natural Causes............................. 138

God Show Us the Way Home 141

Christmas And Feeling Special.. 143

The Meaning of a Handshake 145

Believe The Magic of Christmas 147

Revitalization of Life Memories 148

Just How Honest Will He Be... 150

Raging Out Of Control.. 152

In Our Time of Need 154

The Basics of Life in a Recession 156

I Call It Gods Plan for the Future 158

A Publishers Dream an Authors Nightmare.............................. 160

Failure In the Family Department... 162

Sometimes Things Are Better Left Unsaid................................. 164

What Do You Want from Me... 166

Ultimatum 168

Re Your All Your Books 170

A Letter About the Author's First Book 171

The Unorthodox Poet: Garry Gosney 172

One Aussies Endeavours Vol 2 Desires Memories Dreams
Lyrics 173

"UNORTHODOX - CONTROVERSIAL - UNCONVENTIONAL"

Other Books by the Author

Perth Desperado
Aka:
Garry William Gosney

My website address

www.a-world-of-poetry.com
http://www.angelfire.com/wv2/PerthDesperado/index.html

Out Now
"ONE AUSSIE'S ENDEAVOURS"
Poetry   Writings   Lyrics   Feelings

Out Now
"CONTRAVERSIAL" – part 1 and 2
Dreams   Wishes   Hopes   Lyrics

Out Now
" ONE AUSSIES ENDEAVOURS vol 2 "
Desires   Memories   Dreams   Lyrics

Out Now
"UNORTHODOX My Hearts"
Wishes   Loves   Prayers   Lyrics

Out Now
"CHRISTMAS"
Poetry   Wishes   Feelings   Lyrics

Out Now
"UNORTHODOX CONTROVERSIAL UNCONVENTIONAL
POETRY LYRICS "

GARRY GOSNEY

Winter Storms and Firelight

Winter storms and firelight
Snowflakes drifting in the winter winds
Dinner just for two by candlelight
Soft music playing in the background
...
Snowflakes drifting in the winter winds
Sitting by an open fire roasting chestnuts
Listening to soft music by the firelight
Dinner just for two by candlelight
...
Toasting marshmallows on an open fire
Watching chipmunks playing in the snow
Seeing snowflakes fall through the window
Watching children playing in the snow
...
Snowflakes drifting in the winter winds
Winter storms and firelight
Soft music playing in the background
Toasting marshmallows on an open fire
...
A sign that Christmas is upon us once again
A sign that another year has come to pass
A sign to give thanks and Christmas cheer
A sign to open up our hearts and rejoice
...

"UNORTHODOX - CONTROVERSIAL - UNCONVENTIONAL"

Snowflakes drifting in the winter winds
Winter storms and soft music for two
Roasting chestnuts on an open fire
Watching snowflakes fall in the Christmas wind
The Ghost Whisperer
I hear a whisper but I cannot see
I hear a voice but whose can it be
I see a shadow in the distance
I see and hear it talk to me

...

I close my eyes hoping it would go away
But it only gets stronger and stronger
Its like a mystical mist that wont go away
It's like a mystical wind blowing stronger

...

Chills a shiver that can not be explained
A tear that comes but it cannot be explained
A chill or shiver that comes for no reason at all
A voice or a shadow that comes for no reason at all

...

What could they be trying to tell me or show me?
Just what is this mystical feeling I have in me
Is it my shadow trying to show me the way to go?
Is it my voice trying to whisper the way to go?

...

GARRY GOSNEY

Just what is it that I can hear but cannot see
Just whose shadow is it that I can just see?
Where is this mystical mist coming from?
Why is this mystical feeling getting stronger?
...
Mystical feelings where do they come from
Mystical mist and winds appearing out of nowhere
Mystical voices and shadows where do they come from
Mystical chills and shivers appearing out of nowhere
...
Is it a ghost whispering its needs or asking for help?
Or is it me thats the ghost whisperer

"UNORTHODOX - CONTROVERSIAL - UNCONVENTIONAL"

The Storytellers

The storytellers of the spoken words
The unorthodox words turn into stories
The controversial issues turned into song
The unconventional words turned into poems

...

Words without meanings but with a story
Words that can define a life style
Words that describe a history of nation
Words that bring meaning to heart and soul

...

The storytellers of the spoken words
The unorthodox words turn into poems
The controversial issues turned into stories
The unconventional words turned into song

...

These are the makings of the storytellers
The storytellers of yesteryear and now
They breed life into it as only they can do it
They make you laugh and cry or sad and happy

....

They are the storytellers of the spoken words
Of the unorthodox words turn into stories
Of the controversial issues turned into song
Of the unconventional words turned into poems

....

For they are the storytellers

GARRY GOSNEY

Realestate Agents and Landlords

Realestate agents and landlords
The twist and turns of renting
The landlords are useless the pass the buck
The realestate agents pass the buck too
Neither one want to take responsibility for anything

....

Each one is more corrupt than the police force
Each one more corrupt then the medical, insurance professions
Each one more corrupt then the law system = courts, lawyers,
Each one more corrupt then the local, state, federal government
Each one more corrupt than the local, state, federal politicians

.....

Realestates and landlords and the law
What a combination of corruption more twist and turns than a tornado
But at least you can get a laugh out off the corruption in knowing it
Knowing that the landlords and the realestate agents buck passes
Knowing that they all lie through there teeth even in there asleep

....

They are all out to make a buck but none want the responsibility
They all pass the buck so nothing gets done but buck passing
They all say they want more and give you bills for things on paper
They all pass the buck but nothing is set out clearly just confusion
Not one of them know how to read a gas and power meter at all

....

6

"UNORTHODOX - CONTROVERSIAL - UNCONVENTIONAL"

But guess what they each get one properly done
But no one can copy it out so it's professionally ready
It takes time but they have no commonsense to do it the right format
They think their tenants are just second rate people with no brains
So what do they care for they are corrupt and we all know it

....

Realestate agents and landlords with more twists than a Texas tornado

GARRY GOSNEY

Is It Reincarnation Or Destiny

Where do they come they go
But where do we come from
Better yet where do they go
Is there a before life
Is there an after life
...
Just where do they go
Is there a place we don't know about?
Is there such a place full of happiness
Is it just a fragment of our imagination?
Just where do they go
...
We are born into uncertainty
We are brought into this world what for
What is our journey suppose to be
What is our destiny in life
Is it born to live just to die
...
Is there such a thing as reincarnation
Is there an after life of better things
Have you ever gone somewhere unknown?
Only to find out you had been there before
Is it reincarnation or destiny
...
Just where do they go
Is there a place we don't know about

"UNORTHODOX - CONTROVERSIAL - UNCONVENTIONAL"

Is there such a place full of happiness
Is it just a fragment of our imagination?
Just where do they go
Steve Irwin a Larrikin and Living Legend
Today an icon a living legend passed away
He was a wildlife preserver like no other
He lived life to the fullest like no other could
He was a larrikin like no other we ever had
He was the Australian wildlife larrikin

He brought the world to Australia
He brought Australia to the world
But more importantly than life itself
He brought the world to the world
He was the crocodile hunter with a difference

Crocs rule and natures wildlife at its best criky
Movies and documentaries history in the making
Nature reserves given a new release of life
Education at its best through the eyes of a larrikin
An aussie icon a legion in his own lifetime
He was nature's wildlife larrikin and an ambassador
...
May the larrikin live on forever more
May we remember nature's ambassador
May we cherish the bravery and love of life
May we learn from one of the best of wildlife officers
May Steve Irwin live in the eyes of family and friends

GARRY GOSNEY

...

Today a friend of wildlife passed away
Today let us pray his life has meaning
Today the world animals lost as friend
Today a family lost a friend and confidant
Today Australia lost a son and the world lost a friend

...

condolences to a legend and his family

"UNORTHODOX - CONTROVERSIAL - UNCONVENTIONAL"

What Do You See in Me

What do you see a bum on the street
What do you see a bum with no soul
What do you see a bum with no heart
What do you see a man down on his luck
Just what do you see in tattered clothing
....
You ever thought the bum on the street has a heart
You ever thought the bum on the street has a soul
Ever thought the person in tattered clothing can laugh and cry
Ever thought that what you see is not necessarily so
Just what do you see in the bum on the street
....
Ever taken the time to talk to the bum on the street
Ever taken the time to listen to them speak
Ever taken the time to understand them from the inside
Ever taken the time to see they are a member to someone
That they are someone's son, daughter, mother, father, brother
....
Just what do you see in me a bum on the street without a soul
What do you see in me a bum with no heart in tattered clothes
What do you see in me a bum that is not aloud to laugh and cry
What do you see in me a bum down on his luck or a human
What do you see in me

GARRY GOSNEY

Take Me Back

Take me back to where I belong
Mountain hideaways to watch the world pass by
Mountain mist to cover the tears I cry
Mountain creeks to wash away these tears
Take me back home to where my heart is safe

...

West Virginia Mountains covered in autumn leaves
Mountain hideaways to watch the deer roam
Mountain mist to hide the loneliness
Mountain creeks filled of heaven scent
Take me back to where I was at peace within

...

Dreams of trout filled streams and creeks
Deer and antelope watching bear fishing the creeks
Dreams of trees covered mountains in snow
Chipmunks and squirrels frolicking in the mist
Take me back to the place I came to love

...

Take me back to where I belong
Take me back to where my heart was safe
Take me back to where I was at peace within
Take me back to the place I came to love
Take me back to where I call home home!

"UNORTHODOX - CONTROVERSIAL - UNCONVENTIONAL"

End of an Era, End of A Legend

This week we close an era
Australia lost two icons with in a week
4th of September my daughter's birthday
4th of September croc hunter died
Today is Friday 8th of September in West Australia
King of the mountain 9 times racing champion died
At Gidgegannup in Perth's north-east at about 11:50am (WST).

The legend mobil01 the legion finally put to rest
Peter Brock, Peter perfect, mobil01, king of Bathurst
Call him what you will for you could be right

He was a legend in his own time
He was every Australian males hero and idol
He was every Australian males adrenalin rush
He was the gentleman of the racing circuit
He loved and lived and taught racing when ever he could
Special he wasn't at least not in his eyes
He was an ordinary man living his dream to the fullest
He taught others to be the best they can be
He inspired more than he ever new was humanly possible

GARRY GOSNEY

End of an era
This week Australia lost 2 heroes and 2 icons
Each one special in their own way
Each one was a teacher and a leader in their profession
Each one was larger than life
Each one loved and lived life to the fullest
V8, supper cars, rally cars, will be missing the legend
King of the mountain peter Brock

We hereby knight you " Sir Peter Brock" king of the mountain
You made racing what it is today a delight to watch
You brought auto racing into the homes of Australian people
You showed us that a dream could be achieved at any cost
Not only once you filled your dream but also you did it 9 times
For that " Sir Peter Brock"
I and Australia and the rest of the world thank you
Long live the king of the mountain long live the king
What a sad week for Australia we will never forget you

"UNORTHODOX - CONTROVERSIAL - UNCONVENTIONAL"

Lest We Forget 9/11 2001

Another year has come to pass
9/11 and 5 years later we still feel the pain
We are still at loss as to the reasons why
It's a memory that will never fade or die
9/11 2001 a bit of each of us died that day
...

5 years and the memories still are strong
Strong as if it only happened yesterday
So many questions still remain but no answers
So much pain and suffering from loss of love ones
9/11 2001 a bit of each of us died that day
...

Fireman, police, emergency service did the best
Volunteers, unknown strangers united as one
They did not question should I or shouldn't I
They jumped in not knowing if they could be next
They gave their life for others by helping others
...

9/11 2001 a bit of each of us died that day
The question remain will we ever understand why
We pray for answers and help in understanding
We pray for those that helped a stranger that day
We pray for love-ones that lost their lives
We pray for the families they left behind
...

GARRY GOSNEY

Lest we forget 9/11 2001
For a bit of each of us died that terrible day
Lest we forget 9/11 2001
Fireman, police, emergency services, volunteers
Unknown strangers all united as one
Lest we forget 9/11 2001 the memories
The memories of loves lost needlessly

Unorthodox Controversial Unconventional

My unorthodox love
My controversial heart
My unconventional mind

These are the things I love about life
Each day is unpredictable as the sunrise
Each night is unpredictable as the sunset
Each tide is unpredictable as the oceans

These are the things I love about you
Waking up each day to a new morning of sunrises
Seeing the stars light up the night sky
Seeing the sunrise over the mountain

These are the things I cherish the most
The mystery of your ever-changing land
The mystery of your controversial seasons
The mystery of your unorthodox love for nature

My unorthodox love
My controversial heart
My unconventional mind

GARRY GOSNEY

Friendship... What is Friendship?

F = freely given
R = relationship between others
I = institution
E = establishment
N = no obligation
D = desire
S = should never be under estimated
H = honesty
I = intrust
P = priceless

Friendship what is friendship
Friendship is made up of a lot of thing
It can be with the ones you work with
It can be with the ones you meet on the street
It can be with your neighbours
It can be with people over the net

Friendship is the most used and abuse but why
Your boss is the abuser of friendship for greed
They forget the work place is 30 percent friendship
They forget the work place is 30 percent enjoyment
They forget the work place is 40 percent wages

"UNORTHODOX - CONTROVERSIAL - UNCONVENTIONAL"

Friendship is friends helping friends in time of need
Working longer hrs when they know they should be home
Friends putting their time on hold to lend a helping hand
Friends giving up a fishing trip for a friend
Friends are people who care 24/7 all year around

Friendship is worth all the gold in the world
Friendship is priceless for it is freely given
Friendship is often used and abused
Lend a helping hand to a stranger and become a friend
Open your heart up to a friend instead of abusing them

Friendship is a powerful thing to have
Friendship is a wonderful thing to enjoy
Friendship is a gift of love to others
Friendship what does it mean to you

GARRY GOSNEY

Stop The World

Maybe just maybe the world will stop turning
Maybe the stars won't sparkle any more
Maybe the moon wont glow any more
Maybe the sun won't shine any more
Stop the world from turning I want to get off

Maybe just maybe the world will stop turning
Maybe just maybe I will keep loving you
Maybe the rain will keep falling from above
Maybe the grass will keep growing
Stop the world from turning I want to get off

Maybe just maybe the world will stop turning
Maybe I can learn to play the guitar and sing
Maybe the tide will stop coming in
Maybe just maybe my love for you is real
Stop the world from turning I want to get off

Maybe just maybe the world will stop turning
Maybe the snow will stop falling
Maybe the seasons will stop changing
Maybe the rivers will stop running
Stop the world from turning I want to get off

Things I Miss the Most

Snow capped mountain rangers
Snow drifting in the winter winds
Snow drifting on the open plains
Misty mornings and chilly winds
...
A sign Christmas is in the air
Christmas toys for young and old
Songs full of tears and joy
People sitting around an open fire
...
Snow filled streets all decked out
Streets covered in Christmas lights
Mistletoe hanging in the doorways
Chestnuts roasting on the street corner
...
A sign Christmas is in the air
Christmas presents for young and old
Singing carols in and out of tune
People sipping eggnog around the fire
...
These are the things I miss the most
My children unwrapping there present
Their laughter and joy on the faces
The tears in their eyes through happiness

GARRY GOSNEY

Happy Trails

Country dancing and country songs
Open rangers and cattle trails drives
Cowboys roping and branding in the dust
Cowboys singing by the campfire light
...
Sing along cowboy whistle a merry tune
Sing songs of trail rides long past
Sing songs of cowboys young and old
Singing yippy I aye yippy I ho
Ride em hard, ride em slow, and ride em
...
High plains drifter or cowboy on the move
Rugged mountain rangers a cowboys heaven
Copyboys dancing and singing in the saloon
Copyboys singing to themself in the moonlight
...
Sing along cowboy whistle a merry tune
Sing songs of trail rides long past
Sing songs of cowboys young and old
Singing yippy I aye yippy I ho
Ride em hard, ride em slow, and ride em
...
Hot and dusty summer cattle drives
Winter snow and cold winter winds
Early morning frost along the creek
Cowboys sleeping under the stars

"UNORTHODOX - CONTROVERSIAL - UNCONVENTIONAL"

...
Cowboys singing yippy I aye yippy I yo
yippy I aye happy cattle trails we go

GARRY GOSNEY

The Old Oak Tree

Sitting under the old oak tree
Looking out over the river bank
Listening to sounds of the water
Watching the fish swim on by
...
Sitting under the old oak tree
Watching the clouds roll on in
Dreaming of things that might have been
Dreaming of things won and lost
...
Sitting under the old oak tree
Thinking of just how my heart really feels
Thinking of things that should have been
Thinking of things past and present
...
Sitting under the old oak tree
Thinking, dreaming and listening
Listening to the tails of the old oak tree
What a story he has to tell

"UNORTHODOX - CONTROVERSIAL - UNCONVENTIONAL"

Merry Christmas Everyone

Winter snow flakes and foggy mountain mist
Chilly winds whistling through the trees
Jack frost is in the air tonight
Chipmunks and squirrel hiding in the trees
All signs Christmas time is near once again

...

Long hot summer nights and dry open plains
Hot winds whistling through the trees
The westerly doctor is in the air tonight
Kangaroos and emus hiding under the trees
All signs Christmas is near once again

...

Northern winds filled with winter snow
All sitting around the fire drinking egg nog
Southern winds filled with scorching heat
All standing around the bbq having a cool one
Never the two winds shell meet but it's Christmas

...

Tonight we all come together one and all
We celebrate with love ones near and far
Winter snow, chilly winds and mountain mist
Long hot summer days and dry open plains
All signs that Christmas is here once again

...

GARRY GOSNEY

May God bless you one and all this festive season
May your Christmas be blessed with laughter and joy
Just one last request let us pray for a minute for
For those away from home for what ever the reason
May God protect them from harm and bring them home safely
...
Merry Christmas everyone where ever you are

"UNORTHODOX - CONTROVERSIAL - UNCONVENTIONAL"

Living a Dream Playing Out a Nightmare

He lives a dream he had as a child
As an adult he's playing out a nightmare
He asked for nothing as a child but to dream
He asks for nothing but to live his dream
But all he is now doing is playing out a nightmare
...
He travelled the land of his childhood dreams
A reality that became a dream come true
He travelled and opened his heart up to her beauty
He saw the reality in the beauty of his dreams
He saw the beauty of the land and all she had to offer
...
He travelled the land of his childhood dreams
He was overwhelmed by what he was seeing and experiencing
He was very naive when it came to travelling other countries
Only to have someone turn it into a nightmare a living hell
A reality that was turned into a living nightmare instead
...
He travelled the land of his childhood dreams
He travelled and opened upped his heart to all her beauty
He didn't want or expect much he was happy living a dream
He lived the dream to the best he could loving her beauty
Every river, every mountain, every corner left him in awe
...

GARRY GOSNEY

Now all he is doing is living a dream playing out a nightmare
Reliving the great times he had in his dreams day and night
Reliving the abuse he had in his nightmares day and night
Every photo he took and voice he hears is now a living dream
Every photo he took and voice he hears is now playing out a nightmare

...

Living a dream playing out a nightmare just how will it end
Living a dream playing out a nightmare just when will it end

"UNORTHODOX - CONTROVERSIAL - UNCONVENTIONAL"

Australia My Heart Australia My Home

From the Pacific Ocean to Indian Ocean
From the Murray Darling to the Ord river
From Timor Sea to Great Australian Bite
From sunrise to sunset everything in between
Australia my heart Australia my home

...

Australia the land of vast open plains
Kangaroos, emus and kookaburras laughing
Australia the land of golden sand beaches
From the red sandy desert to the oceans
From to the mountains to the dry dusty plains

...

From the Pacific Ocean to Indian Ocean
From the Murray Darling to the Ord river
From Timor Sea to Great Australian Bite
From sunrise to sunset everything in between
Australia my heart Australia my home

...

Looking up at the Southern Cross by night
To looking at the Great Australian Bite
From Perth to Darwin to Brisbane to Melbourne to Hobart
From Sydney to Adelaide and everything in between
Australia my heart Australia my home

God bless you Australia my heart my home

GARRY GOSNEY

Yesterday Dreams - Todays Fantasy - Tomorrows Reality

They say live for now and plan for now
Live within the real world of now
They say everything else is a fantasy
Reserve you fantasies for your tomorrow
Tomorrow is a dream in the making
So live and plan for today and make it real

Dream for today for tomorrows dream can never be real
Dreams are only wishes your heart make
Today's dream or yesterdays nightmare all can be real
Dreams of the future is a desire the heart makes
The fantasies of today tomorrow's reality and joy

Lets all try to make our dream come true
Make the most of your fantasies for they are your dreams
Don't ever put down another's dream or fantasy
It's the dreams and fantasies of today that can come true
For yesterdays dream and todays fantasy are tomorrows reality

Don't let anyone tell you differently live your dream

"UNORTHODOX - CONTROVERSIAL - UNCONVENTIONAL"

Still Playing Let's Pretend

Another time and place would things be different
Or is it just a case same old stuff different tune
Would all the turmoil in the world be different
Or is it that we are starting to sing a different tune

The world keeps on tuning and the fighting keeps on
Nature keeps crying out loud but is anyone listening
The world keeps on turning and nature keeps crying
Wind, fire and water all crying out the earths is troubled

Another time and place could things be a little different
Would the world be crying out for help in her hour of need
Would the little things we do now really make a difference
Would we have the courage to help mother earth in her need

Another time and place would things be different
Or is it just a case same old stuff different tune
Would all the turmoil in the world be different
Or is it that we are starting to sing a different tune

Are we waking up to senseless needless destruction of the world
Are we waking up or is it just playing let's pretend all is well
Are we waking up to the abuse from governments and business alike
Another time and place but still playing lets pretend all is well

Hear the call the world is hurting

GARRY GOSNEY
April 16th massacre 2007

April 16 a day no different than any other day
Same as any other Monday after a good weekend
Time to hit the schoolbooks or back to work
Everything started off normally it was a great feeling

Everything started off normally like any other day
Every bodies mind was on the tasks of the day ahead
Meeting friends they had not seen over the weekend
Everybody catching up on the weekend gossip and parties

Everything started of normally like any other day
Then to everyone's surprise they was caught up in a deadly rampage
They tranquillity was destroyed by a deadly shooting rampage
Bullets flying every which way they can but why oh God why

Oh God why, Oh God why will I be next what did I do Oh God help us
No where to escape the deadly on slaughter of bullets flying
Reviving memories of Columbine High School massacre in 1999, killed 12
The deadliest shooting US history was in Killeen, Texas, in 1991, 23 killed
1966 at the University of Texas at Austin where 16 killed
2007 at Virginia Tech 32 people killed for no apparent reason at all

Everything started off normally it was a great feeling
Everything started off normally like any other day

"UNORTHODOX - CONTROVERSIAL - UNCONVENTIONAL"

Then to everyone's surprise they was in the middle of bullets flying
Oh God why, Oh God why did this massacre have to happen today
God help us

Why were guns aloud to enter the school campus in the first place
Thousands of questions without answers when it comes to a life
A life that God indented to grow old and teach others the art of life
Thousands of questions first being why are teenagers allowed guns on campus

The best thing we can do is build a monument to honour them all who died today
Lives were taken today God please be kind to them and let them rest forever more
God please help the powers to be to change the gun laws and stop this killing
God please show the powers to be away to find a solution to save lives all life

As to God all life is precious and to God we are all his children

GARRY GOSNEY
0.3842 Cents A Life

What is the total cost of a life I really wonder
From what I see the government say not much

It cost a lot to raise a life
It cost a lot to educate a life
It cost a lot to see a life play
It cost a lot to hear a life laugh and cry

Just what is a life really worth I wonder
We hear of guns killing people everyday
We hear of the odd one or two, three or four
But no-one really takes any notice of them
We hear of 10 to 20 or more and everyone's awake
Even the politicians jump up and say sorry for your loss
But are they really, are they sorry enough to make a change

Is a life the true cost of a 75cent bullet I hope not
Winchester 38 Special Rounds Per Box:50 Box MSRP: $19.21
Sorry I was wrong it is only worth 0.3842 cents per life
Lets put it down to money terms for everyone to understand
1 bullet = 0.3842 cents that makes a human life worth =0.3842

"UNORTHODOX - CONTROVERSIAL - UNCONVENTIONAL"

A bullet here a bullet there a life here a life there
Just how many bullets and lives at 0.3842 cents does it take
Just how many to wake up that a bullet is a life taker
A life of a loved one, a son, a daughter, mother, father
Are they really worth 0.3842 cents or 0.7684 cents if it takes 2

86 people died in campus shootings that = 0.3842x86 = $31.8886
Or 86 people died in campus = 0.7684x86 =$66.0824 PLUS SALES TAX
And all the government can do is say I'm sorry for your loss
It just goes to show just how much a life is worth without TAX
A laugh, a tear, a smile, a life is only worth 0.3842 cents
Even the politicians jump up and say sorry for your loss
But are they really, are they sorry enough to make a change

When will someone say enough is enough God I hope it's soon
Zero tolerance to guns does not mean no guns at all it just means
Tougher gun laws, no guns in cars, no guns without a valid reason
Tougher jail time for offenders but no guns on school grounds policed
No guns unless your on a farm, no guns unless your a member of a club
NOT TOO MUCH TO ASK FOR A LIFE WORTH 0.3842 cents IS IT
..

GARRY GOSNEY

The Colours of Change the Colours of Joy

Fall is now upon us once again
A sign of the times showing changes to come
Leaves falling in their splendid array of colour
Reds, golden browns, yellows and orange
All giving the earth a new look

...

It's just another season to some
To some it has meaning and a purpose
It can breed life into uncertainty
Is it a good thing or a bad thing
No one really knows as it's personal

...

Red for the sunrises and sunsets
Golden brown for the crops in the fields
Yellow for the sunlight and moonbeams
Orange just one of the colours of fall
All giving the earth a new look

...

Fall is upon us once more
Sign winter that is not to far way
The joys of winter laughter in the air
The signs wishes of better things to come
The colours of change the colours of joy

"UNORTHODOX - CONTROVERSIAL - UNCONVENTIONAL"

Oh Snow Beautiful Snow Lovely Winter Snow

Winter chills and snowball fights
Sleigh rides and snow castles
Shadows of snow covered trees
Reindeer prancing in the snow

...

Christmas time is upon us once more
Snow time in the Rockies once again
Telling us all that Christmas is near
Snow covered peaks drifting in the wind

...

Snowflakes falling softly to the ground
Snow crunching under ones footsteps
Oh snow beautiful snow lovely winter snow
Snow flakes falling softly to the ground

...

Listening to soft music and candlelight
Watching snowflakes gently hit the window
Oh snow beautiful snow lovely winter snow
Falling ever so gracefully on my window

GARRY GOSNEY

Six Years on And More to Come

*Six years on and more to come
Six years of memories in the making
Six years of regrets or is it
Six years of memories good and bad
Six years of wondering if only we had
...
Memories of the laughter of yester year
Memories of joys and sorrows together
Walking in the park hand in hand
Singing out off tune to the radio
Watching movies and the soaps on TV
...
Six years of looking at pictures on the wall
Six years of wondering what could have been
Six years of pain and anger of why us Lord
Six years of prayers and unanswered questions
Six years of past and present memories
...
Six years of undivided love
Six years of undivided devotion
Six years of continuous prayers
Six years of memories good and bad
Six years on and more to come*

Things Life Taught Us

Time has come for thanks
Time one refects over the past year
Time one counts his blessing for the good
Time for remembering the good and bad

....

Thanks for the little things life has to offer
Thanks for the laughter, joy and tears we share
Thanks for patter of little feet around the home
Thanks for all the memories good and bad

....

Thanks for all the bad things that life taught us
Thanks for tears that we shed in times of need
Thanks for the chance to learn from our mistakes
Thanks for the second chance at living life again

...

Thanks master for the teaching of life and all it has to offer
Thanks master for the begging of time without end
Thanks master for the days turning into nights into days
Thanks master for the seasons and all their splendour

GARRY GOSNEY

Sing Sing

Sing sing a sweet melody a lullaby
Listen to the sounds of angel singing
Sing sing a sweet melody a lullaby

...

Sing of all things good
Sing of fairies dancing in the garden
Sing of angles in the making
Sing of all things beautiful
Sing of angels flying on gossamer wings

...

Sing sing a sweet melody a lullaby
Listen to the sounds of angel singing
Sing sing a sweet melody a lullaby

...

Sing of the mist on a mountaintop
Sing of mustangs roaming free
Sing of freedom and liberty for all
Sing of love for all things big and small
Sing songs of joy and peace to the world

...

Sing sing a sweet melody a lullaby
Listen to the sounds of angel singing
Sing sing a sweet melody a lullaby
Sing sing like the heavenly choir sing
Sing sing a sweet melody a lullaby

"UNORTHODOX - CONTROVERSIAL - UNCONVENTIONAL"

El Dorado El Dorado My El Dorado

El Dorado a place where I want to be
A place known only unto me
A place where my heart is now living
A place where my mind goes without me
A place called El Dorado

....

A place with sun sets of golden splendour
Mountains full of mist and mystery
The plains covered in golden hue
Creeks flowing steadily to the oceans
Mustangs and buffalo forever free
This is my El Derado

....

El Dorado a place where I want to be
A place known only unto me
A place where my heart is now living
A place where my mind goes without me
A place called El Dorado

....

An imaginary place of great wealth and opportunity
A place where everyone is of even value
A place where opportunity is there for everyone
El Dorado known only to my heart and me
El Dorado where my mind goes without me
This is my El Dorado my El Dorado of tranquillity

GARRY GOSNEY

Pass It on to All Mankind

The power of the people
The powerful voice of one
The power of pass it on
The power of a friendly smile

....

Hold out a friendly hand and say G'day "pass it on "
Give a hug or friendly smile and say "pass it on"
Give 5 minutes to listen to as stranger "pass it on"
Help a friend in need and say thanks "pass it on"

....

The power of the people
The powerful voice of one
The power of love for all mankind
The power of a friendly smile

...

Pass it on pass on a gift of love
Pass on the words of kindness
Pass on a smile to a stranger
Pass on an open hand to someone in need
Pass on friendship to all mankind

"UNORTHODOX - CONTROVERSIAL - UNCONVENTIONAL"

Traditional Christmas

Do you believe in the Christmas spirit?
Do you believe in the joys of Christmas?
Do you believe in the sorrows of Christmas?
Do you believe in the tradition of Christmas?
In just 2 words "I do" believe in all the above

Christmas sorrow for the lost of loved ones
For the lost of all that can not make it home
For all those that have no-one to share Christmas
For the young and old that lost the Christmas spirit
In just 2 words "I do" believe in all the above

Believe in the Christmas spirit and all it has to offer
Believe in the joys Christmas and all they have to bring
Believe in the Christmas wind and the stories it tells
Believe in the laughter floating in on the Christmas wind
In just 2 words "I do" believe in all the above

Do you believe in the tradition of Christmas?
Of giving gifts to others and expecting none in return
Of watching children smiling with joy opening there presents
Of watching the elderly smile or cry over there presents
In just 2 words "I do" believe in all the above

GARRY GOSNEY

The Christmas spirit is in your heart
The Christmas spirit is floating in the air
The Christmas spirit is for young and old alike
The Christmas spirit is for all to enjoy
The Christmas spirit of time in the snow
The Christmas spirit with time at the beach
In just 2 words "I do" believe in all of the above and more

"UNORTHODOX - CONTROVERSIAL - UNCONVENTIONAL"

Northern Lights of Christmas

Northern lights of Christmas shinning brightly
The northern winds spreading Christmas cheer
The mountain winds spreading Christmas snow
All doing their part for the festive season

Children yelling Christmas is near
Shop windows displaying Christmas sales
Parents doing their last minute shopping
Will it be a white Christmas or not
Will the angels sing song of joy and peace?

Northern lights of Christmas shinning brightly
The northern winds spreading Christmas cheer
The mountain winds spreading Christmas snow
All doing their part for the festive season

Young and old giving praise of thanks
Thank you God for the true meaning off Christmas
Thank you God for the greatest gift of all
Thank you God for sending us your son
Thank you God for sharing this day with us

Northern lights of Christmas shinning brightly
The northern winds spreading Christmas cheer
The mountain winds spreading Christmas snow
All doing their part for the festive season

GARRY GOSNEY

Will the angels bless us with songs of joy and peace?
Will the northern lights of Christmas shinning brightly
Will the northern winds spreading Christmas cheer
Will the mountain winds spreading Christmas snow
Will the angels sing songs of praise?

Christmas in The Bush

Country Christmas wide-open spaces in the bush
Bbq and drinking beer and eggnog under a tree
Kookaburras and cockatoos singing in the trees
Koalas and kangaroos watching on from a distance

Family and friends playing childish games
Singing Christmas carols around the bbq
Thongs, shorts and singlet and a cowboy hat
Any thing goes at a country Christmas in the bush

Guitar in hand and good fun to be had by all
Laughing and joking around the picnic table
Telling stories of childhood Christmas of the past
Watching animals basking in the sun from a distance

Children playing and laughing with their presents
Grandparents sleeping in the shade of an old gum tree
Parents drinking and watching the children playing
Country Christmas in the hot Australian summer sun

GARRY GOSNEY

Christmas Memories

*Christmas tree, bright lights and tinsel
Everyone drinking eggnog by the firelight
Mistletoe and halls decked with holly
People singing carols by candlelight*

*The sights and sounds of the joys of Christmas
Everyone singing their favourite Christmas carols
Christmas lights blinking in the background
Sneaking kisses under the mistletoe*

*Snow flakes falling ever so gently
Reindeer frolicking in the snow
Children bobbing for apples in a bowl
The beauty of Christmas at Christmas time*

*Each Christmas is a memory to cherish
Each memory special for whatever the reason
Loss of a love one or a baby's first Christmas
Christmas memories there for the taking*

*Christmas tree, bright lights and tinsel
Snow flakes falling ever so gently
Children bobbing for apples in a bowl
Sneaking kisses under the mistletoe*

"UNORTHODOX - CONTROVERSIAL - UNCONVENTIONAL"

All Christmas memories in the making
All Christmas memories there for the taking
All Christmas memories all cherished memories
It's the most wonderful time of the year

GARRY GOSNEY

Santa is Here

Turn the light out Santa is coming
Close your eyes and go to sleep
Christmas night is here now
Close your eyes my little one

Sweet dreams it is Christmas night
Leave out the milk and cookies
No peeking now Santa is here
Jingles and jangles on the roof

Turn the light out Santa is coming
Close your eyes and go to sleep
Christmas night is here now
Close your eyes my little one

Presents being placed under the tree
Some big and some small some odd shapes
No peeking now Santa is here
What will he leave for you under the tree?

Turn the light out Santa is coming
Close your eyes and go to sleep
Christmas night is here now
Close your eyes my little one
Santa is here

"UNORTHODOX - CONTROVERSIAL - UNCONVENTIONAL"

My Man

You ask for nothing but you give everything
I give you my all for it's all I have
I loves to love and give you my love freely
You're special in every sense of the word
...
You give me far more than I should deserve
You give me love and hope for a better future
You give me far more then I can ever give you
You give me far more then I should ever deserve
...
You are a rebel when you wants to be
You are a saint when you needs to be
You are my joy and sorrows all in one
You are my angel in disguise at all the times
...
You give me far more than I should deserve
You give me love and hope for a better future
You give me far more then I can ever give you
You give me far more then I should ever deserve
...
You're soft and manly when the time is right
You're gentle and a rebel at heart but you're all man
I love you only as I can with all My heart and soul
You ask for nothing except to be my equal my all
...

GARRY GOSNEY

You give me far more than I should deserve
You give me love and hope for a better future
You give me far more then I can ever give you
You give me far more then I should ever deserve
...
You are the man who stole my heart
You are my angel sent from the heavens
You are a dream come true for you are my heart
You are a rebel, you are muscular, and you are all man "my man"
...
You give me far more than I should deserve
You give me love and hope for a better future
You give me far more then I can ever give you
You give me far more then I should ever deserve
...
You ask for nothing except to be my equal my all
You are my equal for you are my reason and my heart
You are my man and I love you so for you are my life
You are my man and my EQUAL love you darlin
My Man

"UNORTHODOX - CONTROVERSIAL - UNCONVENTIONAL"

Just What Are Memories Made Of

Memories just what are memories made of
Family get togethers for birthdays
Family get togethers for Christmas
Family get togethers for holidays
Family get togethers on weekends
...

Celebrating a Childs first birthday
Celebrating a Childs first Christmas
A special time of year for everyone
Time to rejoice for celebrations are near
Celebrations full of joy and Christmas cheer
...

Don't just make money make memories
Money cannot buy health and happiness
Money cannot buy love and joy
Make memories to fill a lifetime
Make memories one can cherish forever
...

For the time to celebrate is right now
The most important time of the year is now
For Christmas is upon us once again
Celebrating the birth of a first child
Not just any child but a child of Christ
...

GARRY GOSNEY

Celebrate the memories and joys of Christmas
Celebrate the Christmas memories and stories
Celebrate and make memories along the way
Making new memories as we go on life's journey
Celebrate for the most wonderful time is now
...
Celebrate the Christmas memories old and new

"UNORTHODOX - CONTROVERSIAL - UNCONVENTIONAL"

Australian Summer

Hot summer days with no relief insight
Hot summer nights hoping for a cool breeze
Spending hot summer days at the beaches
Spending hot summer nights under the fan
Air conditioners working over time
Typical Australian summer hot hot hot

...

Kangaroos and emus hiding under the shade trees
Kookaburras and cockatoos seek shade in the trees
Waterholes sort after by all creatures for coolness
All seeking that ever-elusive cool breeze
Nothing dares move for the sand and sun to hot
Typical Australian summer hot hot hot

...

Over crowded beaches full of people and towels
Children making sandcastles on the waters edge
Adults sitting in the water trying to get cool
Hot summer days with no relief in sight
Nothing dares move for the sand and sun to hot
Typical Australian summer hot hot hot

GARRY GOSNEY

Snowbirds Singing

Snow covered mountains
Snowbirds singing in the treetops
Snow flakes blowing in the wind
Deer roaming through the trees

Children making snowman
Moms and dads decorating the house
Christmas song playing on the radio
Chipmunks watching from the trees

Christmas lights and mistletoe
Snow flakes blowing in the wind
Chipmunks eating peanuts in the snow
Children playing in the snow

Snow covered mountains
Snowbirds singing in the treetops
Christmas songs playing on the radio
Snowbirds singing Christmas is near

"UNORTHODOX - CONTROVERSIAL - UNCONVENTIONAL"

Living Stories

Where do you come from
What do you go to
Where are you running to
What do you want
...

From city boarding schools
From small country towns
Riding horses on a cattle muster
Saddlebags and campfires under the stars
...

Telling stories of times gone by
Living memories in the past
Stories of the past told by the present
Living stories or yester year told today
....

Close your eyes and let your mind go
Think of the things your hear desires
A bed of roses on a deserted island
Drinking pinna coladas under a palm tree

...

GARRY GOSNEY

A Shearer's Life

Shearers out tar boy
Calling wool away sheep o
Click goes the shears one by one
Board boys cleaning the wool away and sweeping
Table hands cleaning the fleece one by one
Wool classer grading the quality of wool
Presser making and branding bales of wool
Shearers calling sheep o pen boy one by one
Cook getting up early to make breakfast and clean
Getting morning smoko ready while making lunch
Getting afternoon smoko ready while making dinner
Up at 4am bed by 9pm the joys of a cook
Shearers up at 5.30 am to start work by 7am
Finish work by 5pm to bed by 9pm what a life
5 days a week work hard, play and drink hard
A shearer's life a hard life but a special breed
A family all rolled into one a life like no other
The bell rings and click goes the shears one by one
Some calling tar and wool away as they go down the shoot
Racing against time trying to beat their own record
Everyone moving to the sound of click goes the shears

"UNORTHODOX - CONTROVERSIAL - UNCONVENTIONAL"

I Wonder Why Maybe So

You will never amount to anything with out me
You will never be happy with out me
You will never sell your books without me
You will never sell your songs without me
All in all you're useless with out me
Your life means nothing with out me
....
I wonder why maybe so
...

You're a paedophile because you talk to kids
Yes I talk to kids my daughter's age why not
They want to know what I write about and live
Your gay or totally incompetent, a faggot
You need to see a Dr your mentally disabled unbalanced
You have a beautiful woman but you don't touch her
...
I wonder why maybe so
...

You say you love me and you want to part of my life
You say you look after me after my operations
You say you're the one that's not out to hurt me
Yet you call me abusive man because I don't touch you
You say I'm abusive because I don't make love to you
You say you know now why my kids don't like me
...

GARRY GOSNEY

I wonder why maybe so

...

You say my poetry books will never sell there no good maybe so
You say I waste my money writing and publishing my books
You say I'm an abusive man not worthy of happiness maybe so
You say I'm incapable of loving any one or letting them close to me
You say I'm impudent, a liar, a cheater, a user and the list is endless
You ask why I don't make love to you or touch you in any way

....

The answer is SIMPLE your ABUSIVE WOMAN and WIFE that why
I wonder why maybe so

...

"UNORTHODOX - CONTROVERSIAL - UNCONVENTIONAL"

Nature At Its Best

Cool winters night all you could hear was an old owl
Singing to the sounds of the wind blowing through the trees
The moon shinning brightly through the tree branches
Chipmunks frolicking through the wet grasses for food
Pinecones and chestnut seeds scattered everywhere

...

Nature's way of saying winter is just around the corner
The owls singing their tunes by night, the birds by day
Deer and chipmunks frolicking in the long grasses
The hint of snow is floating along on the breezes
Seeing the odd snowflake drifting in the wind

...

Nothing escapes the cool breezes that blow
The sounds of the wind whistling through the trees
The beauty of seeing chipmunks and deer frolicking
The beauty of seeing snowflakes in the distance
The sounds of thunder and lightning rolling on in

...

The best time of year to see nature at its best

GARRY GOSNEY

Music is the Universal Language

Beautiful music to listen to
Wonderful music to write to
Slow music to dance to
Soft music to sleep to
Music of love and peace
...
All kinds of music to make the world turn
From country to rock n roll to hip hop
From jazz to blue grass to gospel
From heavy metal to rap and everything in between
Music is the universal language of love and peace
...
Beautiful music to listen to
Wonderful music to write to
Slow music to dance to
Soft music to sleep to
Music of love and peace
...
From farm workers to city office workers
From truck drivers to construction workers
From prisoners to housewife's to ministers
From police to fireman to politician
Music is the universal language of love and peace

"UNORTHODOX - CONTROVERSIAL - UNCONVENTIONAL"

There's A Song Deep Within My Heart

There's a song deep within my heart
There are tears deep within my heart
There's love deep within my heart
Songs of love and tears waiting to surface

...

Songs of joy, laughter and patter of little feet
Of hearing the humming birds amidst the trees
Of deer and chipmunks frolicking in the snow
Of children's laughter filling the town square

...

There's a song deep within my heart
There are tears deep within my heart
There's love deep within my heart
Songs of love and tears waiting to surface

...

Songs of love gone bad or loved ones lost
Of war and tragedy the world all over
Of death and destruction close to home
Of children and the elderly dying in the streets

...

There's a song deep within my heart
There are tears deep within my heart
There's love deep within my heart
Songs of love and tears waiting to surface

GARRY GOSNEY

Spirit of the Mountain

My West Virginia my mountain home
From coal mines and long winding roads
From Marshall football to the mountain Buccaneers
From Hatfield and McCoy's country feuding
...
Wheeling in the north to Williamson in the south
From Morgantown to Martinsburg
From Huntington to White Sulphersprings
From Bluefield to Parkesburg and everything in between
...
A mountain lifestyle like no other
A mountain life others only dream about
A hard ruff and tumble life of the mountainer
Fight hard work hard and love even harder
....
From mountain streams to valley pastures
Mountain top villages to mountain top lakes
To the laughter and joys of the mountain spirit
Autumn leaves to snow covers mountaintops
...
My West Virginia my mountain home
My spirit of the mountain

"UNORTHODOX - CONTROVERSIAL - UNCONVENTIONAL"

When Your Heart Has Left the Building

What do you do when your heart has left
Where can you go to find it again
Just where do you start looking
When your heart has left the building
...

Everything has no meaning or purpose
There is no direction to follow
There is no light to light the way
No meaning, or direction, no light or purpose
...

Where do you go, what do you do
Where do you look for what you cannot see
When your heart has left the building
Where do you go, what do you do
...

The days are long and the nights are even longer
Moon and the stars don't seam to shine anymore
The tears are deep within too deep to surface
Every place you turn a dead end
...

Where do you go, what do you do
Where do you look for what you cannot see
When your heart has left the building
Where do you go, what do you do
....

GARRY GOSNEY

I pray but my prayers never seam to get answered
It like no one is listening to me, like I don't exist
Like I'm a ghost in this house with no place to hide
I pray that someday soon my prayers to be answered

....

What do you do when your heart has left
Where can you go to find it again
Just where do you start looking
When your heart has left the building

...

Everything has no meaning or purpose
There is no direction to follow
There is no light to light the way
No meaning, or direction, no light or purpose

...

Where do you go, what do you do
Where do you look for what you can not see
When your heart has left the building
Where do you go, what do you do

...

The days are long and the nights are even longer
Moon and the stars don't seam to shine anymore
The tears are deep within too deep to surface
Every place you turn a dead-end

...

"UNORTHODOX - CONTROVERSIAL - UNCONVENTIONAL"

Where do you go, what do you do
Where do you look for what you cannot see
When your heart has left the building
Where do you go, what do you do

GARRY GOSNEY

Kentucky Road

Kentucky road take me back to where I belong
Tree covered roads all in different shades of green
Roads winding there way along the mountainside
Mountain tops getting ready for the fall

...

Take me back to the time I felt alive
To the time my heart felt at peace with in
Peace to roam the countryside and enjoy the tranquillity
Or enjoying a stroll with just me and my thoughts

...

Kentucky road take me back to the tranquillity I once knew
Kentucky rain to wash away these tears I shed
Kentucky mist to cover the tears with in
Kentucky mountains full of peace and tranquillity

...

Kentucky woman beautiful as the mountains
Peaceful as the tree covered roads in fall
You bring joy and tranquillity into my life
You bring peace and calm to this old heart of mine

...

Kentucky road take me back to where I belong
Kentucky road take me back to the tranquillity I once knew
Kentucky mountains full of peace and tranquillity
Kentucky bring peace and calm to this old heart of mine

"UNORTHODOX - CONTROVERSIAL - UNCONVENTIONAL"

I Wish I Could Fly

I wish I could be a butterfly
So I would land on a rose petal
I wish I could be a fly on the wall
Then I could listen in on government lies
I wish I could be a bee
Collecting the samples of Mother Nature
I wish I could fly
I would fly to my dreams desires and wishes
Fly over valleys, mountains and streams
Over oceans and deserts and glide on the winds
Fly like the wind and soft like a butterfly
And as cunning as a fly on the wall
Yet fearless as an eagle hovering above
I could fly all over the world
See the world through the eyes of an eagle
See the Seven Wonders of the World
To see the beauty from up above
Marvel at the handy work of our maker's hands
See the destruction of what man left behind
And marvel at God's hands and the power he has
The power the power to destroy the power
The power to build the most beautiful he can
The power the power to give life as only God can
I wish I could fly like my heart does every night
Fly to the beautiful scenery my heart dreams about
God fly me to the beauty you created

GARRY GOSNEY

Please Forgive Me

Teach me to understand the things I don't know
Teach me to understand the things I cannot change
Teach me to understand the ways of the world
Teach me to understand the mysteries of life
But most of all teach me to understand everything about love

...

God give me the power for understanding the things I don't know
God give me the patience to understand everything I don't know
God give me the tolerance to understand what I cannot change
God give me the power to understand the questions I ask
God give me the tolerance to understand the answers I seek

...

God give me the power for understanding the of ways of the world
God give me patience to understand the ways of the world
God give me power to learn the mysteries that life has to offer
God give me the power to understand the questions I ask
God give me the tolerance to understand the answers I seek

...

God give me the power for understanding everything about love
God give me the tolerance I need to find happiness someday
God give me the patience I need to learn more about love
God give me the power to understand the questions I ask
God give me the patience to tolerate and understand the answers I seek

...

"UNORTHODOX - CONTROVERSIAL - UNCONVENTIONAL"

God forgive me for I can not understand the things I don't know
God forgive me for I can not understand why I cannot change things
God forgive me for I can not understand the ways of the world
God forgive me for I can not understand the mysteries of live
God forgive me for I can not understand anything about love

3 Day September 08 Boycott

Its may 2008 and the outcome is not promising at all
The petrol prices in Australia are $1.60 per litre
The price of oil per barrel is $123.oo American
Got told tonight 22 may 08 it will reach 200.00 + a barrel
200.00 plus a barrel by Christmas time 08 what a thought
That will make a minimum price of 7.50 up to 8.25 per gallon
That the price we paid for changing to litres from gallons
The day before we changed over was 80cents a gallon in the early 70s
The next day it went to 80 cents a litre 4.5 times than it should have
1 gallon = 4.54609litres that is 4.54 x the cost per litre for fuel
The only thing that slow the speed of fuel prices is another recession
What is need to wake up the oil giants and the governments is a recession
The depression as big as the 30s/40s will more than do the job
No country can support the highest prices the world has ever seen
The fuel prices have seen a 300 percent in the last 12 mths
The cost of food has gone up 300 percent to help cover the high prices
The pensions have stayed stationary while the inflation up 300 percent
Just how much can one afford before the world stops turning
Petrol out of reach. Food out of reach. Clothing out of reach
The cost of medications out of reach.
The cost of housing both owning and renting getting out of reach
The cost of living is killing people both mentally and physically
Where will it stop? When will we be back to normal prices?

"UNORTHODOX - CONTROVERSIAL - UNCONVENTIONAL"

That is the million-dollar question with no answers in sight

If the government don't / wont do anything then its up to the people

1 good way of doing it is everyone stayed home for 3 days all at once

2 good way of doing it is everyone didn't buy fuel for 3 days all at once

3 if everyone united in every country for 3 days no buying fuel

We would bring the world to its knees over night

The cost of fuel would be 70 percent less then what is now

The companies would have lost trillions of dollars world wide they deserve it

The more they loose the cheaper it gets because they will want us to buy it

It will make both governments and oil giants sit up and listen to the public

The power of 1 the power of the people are many the power of the world public

Well what can one say but power to the people of the world united as one

Do not under estimate the power of the people for their voices will carry

Please Lets try for a 3 day SEPTEMBER 08 boycott of all fuel prices

GARRY GOSNEY

Shared Along the Way

Miles so many miles to the heart I own
So many miles I must travel to my heart
To the heart that left me behind
To my heart travelling without me

So many miles to catch up with the heart I own
So many tears I must cry for the heart I own
So many days and night must pass until united
Northern lights look after the heart you own

Dreams are all I have left of the heart I own
The dreams we share each night as one
The roads travelled all shared with the heart I own
Each mile, hill, tree all shared along the way

Each a memory shared along the way

"UNORTHODOX - CONTROVERSIAL - UNCONVENTIONAL"

A Mother's Prayer

I pray that my sons and daughter stay safe
I pray they get a better chance at life than I did
I pray that someday they will understand me
I pray that the road they travel is easier then mine

But most of all God I pray that they do not come to harm
I pray that each will find their own way to peace and harmony
To remember that they are and always will be loved by me
To remember the lights are always left on for them

I pray the road I take is learning for me
I pray that my children will learn from my journeys
God please keep them safe from everything that is unsafe
God help keep them honest to themselves if no one else

God we all make mistakes but I pray that you forgive us
I pray that you guide us and help us to become better
To become the best mother and father we can be
To become the best children that we know they can be

God please grant my children the wisdom to understand me
Please grant them the patience and tolerance I didn't have
Please God give them the love I did not know how to give
God please teach and help them wherever I cannot
This is my mother's prayer to you

GARRY GOSNEY

A Fathers Love

Drugs the destroyer of families
Brothers and sisters fighting over what is right
Parents' fighting over what is right or wrong
It's even harder when parents have gone separate ways

...

Long distant fathers a phone call away
A stranger without a family fighting for love
A father trying to reach out to a son in need
Has he the right to compete for the sons love

...

All his family and friends are close by he said
Yes they are all there close at hand but were they
Where were they when he was destroying himself?
Just what were they doing just watching and waiting

...

Waiting for drugs to destroy the family more than it was
Fighting who is right or wrong why wasn't something done
Trying to ask questions why they didn't see it coming
Were they occupied with their own needs to see the signs?

...

4000 miles away he gets a call son trying to kill himself
Son put into hospital but not told how when or why it happened
His brothers and sisters try to explain the best they can
His father looking for answers his ex wont give any answers

...

"UNORTHODOX - CONTROVERSIAL - UNCONVENTIONAL"

His mother well what can one say she let him get that way
She never returns phone calls and when she dose she's abusive
That is unless she really wants something then the tears run
Niagara fall watch out her tears are a flowing for she's in need

...

A son calling out for help a father trying from a distance
A fathers love that's unconditional but 4000 miles away
Just what can he do, just what should he do,
The million-dollar question is there anything he can do

...

A father's love that can never be felt
The tears he sheds for the love he yearns to give
Is there a right way or a wrong way to love?
With the pain the father shares with his son ever go away

...

Was he a good father, is he a good father, can he be a good father
Just how will this love end in tragedy or in happiness?
Just how will their love for each other end will they ever be close
Will it end in a father's love that can never be felt?

GARRY GOSNEY

The Question Is Better Asked

Why should we be made to feel like we are second-rate people always getting the royal shaft?

We know we are on a pension but do you think it's too much to ask for a clean place to live

A clean yard and the cockroaches sprayed inside and outside every 6 months professionally

And in the mean time we keep it clean inside and out the best we can the rest of the year

We know we are at the poor end of the rental scale, second-rate so they might say

But we believe a tenant should look after the unit / house / what ever

And the real-estate agents should do there bit too as well as the owners

It's a 3 way street in my book ...

Each looking and working for a common goal and that is decent tenants and decent place

Decent landlords and real-estate agents to listen to our needs and do the maintenance

So that everyone can have pride in the dump where they live.. So to speak of

Not live in a place not even the cockroaches don't want to live in

People can make a million dollar house look like a rubbish dump or worse

People can take a dump of a place and make it look decent and respectable

Poor people have pride too ... and they have dignity too.. They even have respect

Yes some even have respect for what they do not own

Respect is a 3 way street in my book

"UNORTHODOX - CONTROVERSIAL - UNCONVENTIONAL"

Respect for tenants rights to live in a decent place by landlords and real-estate agents

In return tenants should respect other peoples property and things that are there for their use

Everything is not always about the " almighty dollar " good tenants can save you money

Bad tenants can cost you thousands of dollars every time they destroy a property

A unit a cross from me cost 20,000 to rebuild from the floor up

Another one cost 15,000 to rebuild from the floor up how many owners can afford that

The question is better asked how many can afford that 3 to 4 times a year

The question is better asked is it the real-estates agents at fault for letting it happen

The question is better asked do the owners really care or is it just a tax write-off for them

People ask for things to be done around the place just a hand to make thing better

Mostly little things that may cost a bit in the short term but in the long run costs are minor

But months pass of asking the same old questions, then it's like you're talking to a brick walk

We are made to feel like we are inadequate and insufficient so we get the royal shaft

Bureaucracy of he said, she said, I cannot make that decisions; I have to ask, leave it with me

Bureaucratic procedure that is so flawed no-one knows who's the boss or don't want to know

Bureaucratic procedure pass the buck then no one is right and no one is wrong what a joke

Politicians that are afraid to interfere because of " conflict of interest " give us a break

Conflict of interest means there on the take like the police department on the take

We would like to think that there are some good people in places of power

But one thing is for sure none of us will hold our breath thats for sure

Give us our poor peoples pride and dignity back so some of us can live like humans

This is all we ask as tenants yes I know there is a lot that could not give a damm.

I'm the 1st to admit to that and I have photos to prove it but when you have to take an owner

And 1st national realty to court over a doorknob THATS GOING TO FAR

I still have the paper work and the photos from the court case as well

The whole system needs to be overhauled a 1000 percent, but I guess there is always someone

Always someone to stuff it up for the decent poor folk out there that take pride in where they live

Pride is just not for the RICH AND FAMOUS but for EVERYONE

"UNORTHODOX - CONTROVERSIAL - UNCONVENTIONAL"

Oh What A Majestic Sight to See

Snowflakes big and small drifting in the wind
Soft flurries gently drifting to the ground
Snowflakes sitting on the leaves and branches
A gentle coat of snowflakes on the grass

...

Snow covered mountaintops in the distance
Mountain mist moving slowly down the valley
Mountain streams filled with rainbow trout
Mustangs roaming free upon the plains

...

The sights and sounds of seasons changing
Snow covered mountaintops in the distance
Mountain mist moving slowly down the valley
A sign that winter is fast approaching

...

Snowflake falling big and small in the breeze
Everyone preparing for the coming winter
Mustangs roaming free looking for better ground
Flurries starting to come think and fast

...

Mountain mist moving slowly down the valley
Streams filled with trout all looking for a deep pond
Streams starting to ice over as winter starts to sets in
A sign winter is fast settling in

...

GARRY GOSNEY

Snowflakes sitting on the trees
Oh what a majestic sight to see
Sitting by a warm fire looking out the window
Watching snowflakes gentle falling to the ground
...
Oh what a majestic sight to see
Snowflakes falling gently to the ground
Mountaintops, valley and plains all covered in snow
Snowbirds singing merrily in the snow covered trees
...
Oh what a majestic sight to see

"UNORTHODOX - CONTROVERSIAL - UNCONVENTIONAL"

Live Your Dream

Dreams of heavenly things to come
Dreams of the past
Reliving the joys and the sorrows
Can dreams become a reality?
Or is reality a dream come true

...

Daydreamer live your dream
Dream of the things you desire
Dream of happiness and peace

...

Dream of a house with a white picket fence
Of the pitter patter of little feet
Of laughter and love ones near by
Of chandeliers and candlelight dinners

...

Night-time dreamer live your dream
Dream of the things you desire
Dream of happiness and peace

...

Dream of star filled skies
Of full moons and falling stars
Of rainbows and snowflakes
Of laughter around a open fire

...

GARRY GOSNEY

Day-time dreamer live your dream
Dream of the things you desire
Dream of happiness and peace
Night-time dreamer live your dream

"UNORTHODOX - CONTROVERSIAL - UNCONVENTIONAL"

A Woman In The Making

Young girl you will be a woman soon
A baby full of love and kisses
A young girl full of love and mischief
A woman full of love and mysterious ways

...

From carpet crawler to angel biter
Oh how the times changed my baby girl
How you have grown up from baby to pony tails
From a beautiful girl to a wonderful woman

...

Times have change mountains
Times have change my baby girl into a woman
Baby kisses to bobby socks to stockings to a woman
What more could anyone ask for beauty at its best

...

From lullaby's to pajama parties to boyfriends
How the times have changed along with you
From baby to ponytails to a beautiful woman
Young girl you will be a woman soon

...

Mysterious, unpredictable, yet beautiful
All the qualities of your mother
Mysterious, unpredictable, yet beautiful
All the qualities of a mother to be

...

GARRY GOSNEY

What a site to see beauty at its best
Mother nature at her very best
A woman in the making
Girl you will be a woman soon

"UNORTHODOX - CONTROVERSIAL - UNCONVENTIONAL"

My MOM

It was awesome to see mom after 26 years
To see the changes the years have had on her
To see if time and distance would change anything
But nothing had changed at all 2 hrs later ww3

...

World war 3 over money where's my money
Not a week or two to get settled in
But where's my money everyday the same routine
Morning noon and night a lecture on the facts of life

...

Her husband no kids of his own giving a lecture
Asking for money every chance he got
When mom married him she went down hill not forward
He tries to play dad to a 50 year old and it's a joke

...

It was 2 weeks of pure hell and abuse from him
Walking 10 klms into town looking for a place
Walking in and out but it was worth it
We found a place it was ok at short notice

...

18 mths later things did start to come good
Mom and I was getting on great and having fun for once
It lasted 6 months before he went ballistic again
Now it's just down to phone calls and meeting at the shops

...

GARRY GOSNEY

Phone calls and shops is what we are restricted too
I could be 20,000 miles away and still make calls
In Canada or America still only a phone call away
One thing is for sure no one will or can stop me
...
Loving my mom we may have our differences which we do
But no matter what I will never stop loving her
No matter how close or how far apart we are
She is and always will be my mom love you mom

"UNORTHODOX - CONTROVERSIAL - UNCONVENTIONAL"

Picture They Call Life

What is life all about where do I fit into the picture
Is it about how you feel or is it about their feeling
What is it all about do I have a say in this matter
Just where do I fit in this picture they call life

...

Walking down the street getting told where to walk
What side I should walk on, what would people think
Is it all about you, them, us, where do I fit in all this
You say it's all about how others see you through me

...

Talking getting told what to say or not to say
Getting lectures when I get home of what I didn't say or do
You say I am an embarrassment to you by the way I act
You tell me to do this and that so it makes you look good

...

You tell me it's all about how people see you that matters
You tell me it's all about what they think of you that counts
It's all about the perception and mental representation
It's all about you and we must paint a perfect picture of you

...

Just where do I fit into this picture of life if at all
All I see is it is about you, them and family perceptions
Just what will they think, how could you, you never lie
You never lie just what will my family think of me or us

...

GARRY GOSNEY

What is life all about where do I fit into the picture
Is it about how you feel or is it about their feeling
What is it all about do I have a say in this matter
Just where do I fit in this picture they call life

...

Just where do I fit in this picture they call life
What is it all about, do I have a say in this matter
Is it all about you, them and how they see us together
Just what are my rights in all of this game called life

...

"UNORTHODOX - CONTROVERSIAL - UNCONVENTIONAL"

Seven Years of Living Memories

Seven years and still going strong
Seven years and the memories still strong
Memories that stopped a nation in its tracks
Memories that stopped the world with disbelieve

...

Memories of that fatal day ever so strong
The day of plane crashes and buildings falling
The day innocent victims died and hero's was made
11th September 2001 forever remembered

...

A day the world stood still and mourned
Mourned the innocent, the brave and the hero's
World trade center, Whitehouse, plane crashes
All innocent victims raped of their freedom

...

Families destroyed, some even made stronger
For there families have a common denominator
The day innocent victims died and hero's was made
11th September 2001 forever remembered

...

Seven years and still going strong in our hearts
Memories that stopped the world with disbelieve
11th September 2001 forever remembered and honored
A world of innocent victims raped of their freedom

...

GARRY GOSNEY

A nation brought to its knees in horror and disbelief
A world united in prayers on that September day
A world united under one banner for freedom for all
A world remembering the innocent, the brave and the hero's
...
Seven years of living memories of that fatal day
Family's destroyed but everlasting friendships made
God look after and watch over the innocent victims
God we pray for all those that survived that fatal day
God we pray for a world that lost its freedom

.

"UNORTHODOX - CONTROVERSIAL - UNCONVENTIONAL"

The Legacy of the Flag

Fly that flag my child high for all to see
Let the world see it flying high and proud
Show everyone just how proud you are
Show them the glory and honour in the flag

...

Wars come and go also wars maybe won and lost
Everyone believing his or her cause is right
Everyone trying to justify his or her actions
But everyone believing in the dream of freedom

...

Fly that flag my child high for all to see
Let the world see it flying high and proud
Show everyone just how proud you are
Show them the glory and honour in the flag

...

From sunset plains to golden sandy beaches
From snow covered mountains to sandy deserts
From cattle roaming the plains to starry nights
From factory workers to breaking mustangs

...

Fly that flag my child high for all to see
Let the world see it flying high and proud
Show everyone just how proud you are
Show them the glory and honour in the flag

...

GARRY GOSNEY

Fly that flag for all the glory in the world
Be proud in the heritage of the flag my child
Be proud of the legacy the flag leaves behind
Be proud of the glory and honour in the flag
The legacy of the flag

"UNORTHODOX - CONTROVERSIAL - UNCONVENTIONAL"

The Year Is 2008 The Month Is October

The year is 2008 the month October
The month that the richest countries have fallen
Falling from grace as the most powerful nations
But it was a fall they could never see coming
It was a fall of the worst kind it was greed
Greed by the governments and greed by the banks
Greed of multi million dollars wages for nothing
Million dollar wages for bosses of companies that went bust

Governments paying million dollar bailouts that should never have happened
Greed greed and more greed living of the fat of the land and not giving back
People living out side their means and screaming their hard done by
Over priced houses and over priced cars and over priced wages all for what

The year is 2008 the month October
The month that the richest countries have fallen
Falling from grace as the most powerful nations
But it was a fall they could never see coming
It was a fall of the worst kind it was greed
Greed by the governments and greed by the banks
Greed of multi million dollars wages for nothing
Million dollar wages for bosses of companies that went bust

GARRY GOSNEY

Over priced politicians wages and over priced business executive wages

Over inflated banks and over priced companies buying politicians off

Governments turning a blind eye because they were being paid under the table

Big business saying pass this law, pass that law we know what the world needs

...

The year is 2008 the month October

The month that the richest countries have fallen

Falling from grace as the most powerful nations

But it was a fall they could never see coming

It was a fall of the worst kind it was greed

Greed by the governments and greed by the banks

Greed of multi million dollars wages for nothing

Million dollar wages for bosses of companies that went bust

...

But its the little people of this world the poor

That will once again rebuild a nation for they will pick up the fallen

They will hold out their hand and show the fallen all is not lost

They will show them that they can once again rebuild what was lost

...

The year is 2008 the month is October and all is not lost

"UNORTHODOX - CONTROVERSIAL - UNCONVENTIONAL"

The Recession Of Greed

It's been a decade full of ups and downs
A decade of disasters one after another
But mostly a decade of yuppies and flashy cars
Yuppies living the high life with out consequences
Flashy cars and houses and multi credit cards
Spending more than what they could ever earn

...

A decade of disasters one after another
First there was the world trade centre in America
Secondly the war on irac/ Iran and Afghanistan
Thirdly the oil crises that came about because of greed
President bushes greed to monopolize the worlds oil prices
But he tried to lay the blame onto others but failed miserable

...

Forth thing was hurricane Katrina took out New Orleans
Then the best of all a worldwide recession that started with bush
Everything started with the oil prices that sky rocketed through greed
Greed of one man George bush he wanted to set the stage of world dictator

...

But the beauty in all this is the fact America will never again be no 1
He greed backfired on him beautifully as it brought enemies to help out
It have made everyone equal and now its there turn to hold the whip
Everyone has brought in on this man made disaster trying help out
Every country rich or poor every human rich or poor are buying into it

GARRY GOSNEY

...

A decade of disasters but for one reason or another it have been a blessing

Yes a blessing in disguise for everyone have been united under one banner

The banner of the worldwide recession better known as the recession of greed

"UNORTHODOX - CONTROVERSIAL - UNCONVENTIONAL"

Homesick

Homesick thinking of the times he left behind
He was thinking of what could have been
He was thinking of the peace and tranquillity
He dreams of hope of better things to come
He was reminiscing over his heart and all the tears lost
...
He was thinking of the tears his heart is crying for its home
All the tears of sorrow for the country that owns her heart
All the tears of pain for the love he has was ripped out of him
A loss that can never be regained for the damage was so great
He was thinking of the ruff times along the way
...
He was thinking just thinking of the times past and present
Thinking of his desires loves and wonders what might have been
He is always crying tears of sorrow for what should have been
Homesick for his heart to be united once again in peace
Reminiscing of the things he longed for he longed to be back home
...
For he was homesick for the land he loves that stole is heart
For he was homesick for his heart that's travelling the land he loved

GARRY GOSNEY

The Beauty of a Recession

Recession the beauty of a recession
The beauty it the greedy get humbled
The rich loose 75 percent of their wealth
The poor well they stay poor

...

The rich some will lose 75 percent of their wealth
Some will fall to the streets they once walked
Some will commit suicide rightly so through their greed
Some will be given a hand to pick themself up again

...

The recession will not stop until the price of fuel drops
September 08 the oil price per barrel was $149.50+ us a barrel
October 08 the price is $67.40 + USA a barrel but the price is high
The price of fuel did not drop by 60 percent like oil did a barrel

...

Once fuel gets down to 20 cents a gallon and stays there for 2 yrs
Then and only them will the world start to see an improvement
Oil needs to get back to $20.00 us a barrel for 2 yrs and stabilize
The people of the world have spoken their terms of agreement

...

But the oil companies & governments greed will not listen to the people
We know they think they are number one but in fact they are sadly mistaken
Their greed will not be tolerated no longer so the question remains
When will they listen to the words of the people and drop fuel prices

...

"UNORTHODOX - CONTROVERSIAL - UNCONVENTIONAL"

The recession can and only will be stoped when greed no longer exist

Not for a day, not for a year, not for a decade but for a lifetime

This is the turning point that everyone in power should listen to

But will they learn it 2008 or 2009 or 2010 or 2011 or when is the question

...

2010 we hit rock bottom if the fuel price go down and stay down

2012 should see the world stabilize and 2014 should see it getting better

2015 should see best of the best starting up once again

But a lot of businesses will not be there unless they learn to humble themselves

...

GARRY GOSNEY

A Pathetic Place to Live

The world is a pathetic place to live
Governments fighting governments
Governments lying to its people
Business extorting money from everyone who uses them
Business over charging everyone purely for the greed

...

The countries are passing the buck every chance they get
Governments blaming big business every chance they get
Each one blaming each one for climate change, credit crunch
Each one blaming each other for the recession, housing crisis
Each one blaming each other for unemployment, and high prices

...

Just when will the government stop lying to it people
Will big business stop its greed and ripping off the public?
Will stop employing ignorant people that cannot think for themselves
Everyone is scared of putting his or her name on paper or there hand up
No one wants to rock the boat and be made accountable for his or her actions

...

When will governments and their employees ever listen to the public?
When will big business and their employees ever listen to the public?
Each one thinks they are gods gift to the world but their sadly mistaken
The world did not ask for corruption or of the greed it has witnessed
The people of the world only asked for honestly by all involved

...

"UNORTHODOX - CONTROVERSIAL - UNCONVENTIONAL"

But business lies and says they can provide a service when they cannot

Governments lie and say they can provide a service when they cannot

Each one denying they are the guilty party by there ignorance, incompetence

There is not a government depart that is not corrupt due the there ignorance

The police and the legal system are the most corrupt off them all

...

The police abuse the power in everything they do and government condone it

The law society is a joke their over priced and are brought off by insurance companies

And the judge's well there on the take criminal that kills should get life

But don't a teen killer or an adult killer there is only one sentence.. Life

Nothing more nothing less drunk or on drugs is no excuse it's a copout at best

...

The police, sheriffs any law enforcement are noted for planting drugs weapons etc etc

The government and big business condone what they do so they get away with it

There is enough corruption and incompetence in the world without them adding to it

Its time governments and big and small business clean up there act big time

Not just sweep the ignorance and incompetence under the carpet as we all know they do

GARRY GOSNEY

...

When will they Learn

"UNORTHODOX - CONTROVERSIAL - UNCONVENTIONAL"

God Bless The World

The dollar goes up and down like a yoyo
Money woes and economy ups and downs
Credit crunch and work place retrenchments
Stocks, bonds up and down in the share market
Business folding due to the times

...

Just how long will it take to get better?
Just when will things start to stabilize
Just when will the stock exchange stabilize
Just when will the world's turmoil end

...

The dollar goes up and down like a yoyo
Money woes and economy ups and downs
Credit crunch and work place retrenchments
Stocks, bonds up and down in the share market
Business folding due to the times

...

Farmers having to do it tough on the land
Factories torn between foreclosure and staying open
Is it loyalty between the factories and the communities?
Better yet can anyone say who is or what is at fault?

...

Just how did it start I think we all know the answer
But they will never blame the right one the greedy one
But it started with the need for greed on the oil prices
He starts a war to get control of the oil prices

GARRY GOSNEY

...

They call him the greediest president to ever walk the earth
They only president that should be charged with war crimes
But guess what everyone is too scared touch the corruption
For its in all the political ranks from top to bottom

...

God bless the world for god is the only one that can

"UNORTHODOX - CONTROVERSIAL - UNCONVENTIONAL"

Times Have Changed the World

The world is a funny place to say the least

You have politicians running for selection of president for the 1st time

Senators running for of president it's a joke in fact it's a con job

Each is running each other down slandering for a better word

...

But in fact none of them know anything about running a country

So know how to run a state and some don't but that's elections for ya

But in running they promise you the moon because the world is your oyster

They blow sunshine where the sun don't shine and never has and never will

...

They promise you gold but what you get is fools gold and false promises

In reality its not the president that makes the decisions its is staff

The parliament lower house and the upper house make all the decisions

But the president can make a request but its both house he has to convince

...

He has the final say in a few things but reality he's a puppet to his party

The party puts through what it wants and he signs his name to it

But really does he ever read what he signs .. No his staff do it all

Election time is not about the man but about party who can do the best con

GARRY GOSNEY

...

Who is the best man at coning the every day people will win the race

Yes we need a change but change don't happen over night it takes years

Yes years of hard work and a lot of fighting and bickering to make it happen

It's about the yes man that can put up the best fight within the party to win

...

He is in fact an outcast for he stands alone in everything he does

It's his head on the chopping block every day he is in power with everyone watching

His party elected him but in reality they elected a fall guy for anything wrong

But he's family has no privacy at all and everyone pouncing on every word spoken

...

Just who is running the country .. The policy makers .. Houses of parliament

Just where does the leader of the country actually fit into the picture

He signs his name to a piece of paper that he may or may not have read

His chief says sign here because everyone has read it and said it was ok

...

It's a dangerous game to play and a lonely one for you could be hung out to dry

The year of the computer was both a blessing and a disaster but its now reality

No one is safe any more any where for you have " the eye in the sky"

"UNORTHODOX - CONTROVERSIAL - UNCONVENTIONAL"

watching you

Times have changed the world for we can now watch them watching us 24 hours a day

...

GARRY GOSNEY

The World Has Spoken

The recession that was really need and very much welcome..

It was started 20 yrs ago by the greed brought on by BUSINESS and GOVERNMENT GREED.

But 2001 started another kind of war brought on by the American government.

But the biggest war was started 2002 by greed to control the price of oil by American government

2007 another war was started by the American government and its called GREED, GIVE ME !! GIVE ME !!

So now the people have taken over the WAR ON GREED.

It is no longer in the hands of corrupt governments the departments or big business :)

It is now in the hands of the little people of the world ..

This is a war the government and business can not win.

This war is the power of human being the little people of the world

One could say the shit kickers of the world the average person just trying to make ends meet :)

They are the ones that will fight tooth and nail for their rights to be heard.

There is no law of the land that will or can stop us if they try that means they're corrupt

When fuel get down to 30 cents a gallon at the pumps then and only then will we think of listening..

I mean 30 cents a gallon not 30 cents a litre but 30 cents a gallon that means 0.066 cents a litre

All fuel companies and governments must serender their greed and it stays that was for 2 yrs

Then and only then will the worlds little people see its way to clear the way to meet half way

"UNORTHODOX - CONTROVERSIAL - UNCONVENTIONAL"

For the recession to end there is a possibility that 2012 could be the yr to see a way out

But full recovery will 2020 if the government act now ..

If the government and business don't act before 2012 then it could be 2030

Before the little people release the world from it greed ...

There will be no more 1 million dollar wage packets or 80 million dollar wage packages either.

But there will be a lot of business folded and all assets / bank accounts frozen for 30 yrs

If all business bosses and all interest and sales given to who ever they owe money to ..

Workers first then creditors ..

The rules have changed the governments don't make the rules any more :)

This is a WAR a WAR that the little people set and make the rules reason being ..

The governments are to corrupt to make decision that concern the public

So the public must make sure that the governments and big business take note about what we want ..

But we will let the government work it as they are QUOTE " suppose to be highly educated "

But not one of us will hold their breath because it was there coruption that put us where we are now

It was their TRACK RECORD THAT BRED GREED AND PUT US INTO A RECESSION ...something we will never forget.

NOW ITS UP TO US THE GENERAL PUBLIC to dictate the terms and conditions

To make sure we are listened too ..

For we are the ones that will say when the recessions stops not the governments ..

The governments and business started it but we will stop it when our demands have been heard ..

Its simple as STOP THE GREED and in 5 yrs we maybe out of the recession that the governments

and big business brought on

That little people of the world have spoken.. By voting ..

No more greed, no more million dollar wages, no more million dollar retirement packages for anyone.

No more million dollar hand outs for businesses going under, no more million dollar handshakes.

No more greed , no more presidents million dollar retirement fund each yr .. plain and simple

NO MORE GREED BY ANY ONE .. business exe or politions or company owners NO MORE GREED

The citizens of the world have spoken in November 2008 no more greed

"UNORTHODOX - CONTROVERSIAL - UNCONVENTIONAL"

Christmas Recession 2008

Most don't understand what a recession means
"The state of the economy declines;
a widespread decline in the GDP and employment
and trade lasting from six months to a year or many more"
...
We hear the governments sugar coat everything
High on promise low on doing but mostly covering up
Its a time when everything is tight the world over
It's when jobs are lost and business close their doors
7 out of 10 will close their doors for the last time
...
This year 2008 will go down in history as year to remember
A year for the first black president of America and the world
A year was declared a worldwide recession bigger then the 30s
A first Christmas of the great 2008 worldwide recession
This is bigger then the 1930s recession ever was 78 years go
...
Bigger in everyway possible and can not be covered up any more
The worlds first Christmas with out the Christmas spirit
Just what is the Christmas spirit and how will it play its apart
Is it the Christmas spirit bringing us all back to reality?
Back to reality of the true meaning of the Christmas spirit
...

GARRY GOSNEY

Give a hand, give a smile, give a hug, give time to a stranger
Hold out a hand to those less fortunate than ourselves
Ask not what your fellow man can do for you in time of need
But what you can do for your fellow man in time of need
Christmas is about giving from the heart not about receiving

...

This is a lesson in the basics of the Christmas spirit
If you think you have nothing to give your wrong on all accounts
For you have your heart, your friendship, but most of all yourself
The Christmas spirit is alive and well even in a recession
We can still have the Christmas spirit even in a Christmas recession

...

Lets all learn the basic from the Christmas spirit

"UNORTHODOX - CONTROVERSIAL - UNCONVENTIONAL"

Questioning Incompetence

One thing is easy to see and that is incompetence
Incompetence in business is so think you can cut it
They are always trying to pass the blame onto you
But in reality it's there poorhouse keeping that's to blame
...
One thing is easy to see and that is incompetence
Incompetence in government is so think you can cut it
The government departments all try to blame each other and you
But in reality they are to blame for there own idiosyncrasies
...
They are trained to always blame someone else no matter what
The best for that are vehicle insurance companies they set the standard
The standard of corruption anything and everything they can think off
Anything so they don't have to payout for you is the enemy
...
They are perfect and they are right in everything they say and do
They have the law and corruption on there side for they are all on the take
One thing about all business regardless of the size is founded on greed
Government departments regardless of the size is founded on greed
...

GARRY GOSNEY

It's all a cover up for there incompetence to hide their corruption

There own idiosyncrasies mostly because they have no idea what their doing

But their put into a God like position a with a stun mullet attitude

How dare you question me, yes we dare and will continue to do so your no God

"UNORTHODOX - CONTROVERSIAL - UNCONVENTIONAL"
Things We Are Not Suppose To KNOW

Things we are not suppose to know
1. How banks make there millions over night and give you pennies
2. Like how governments and business go hand in hand in greed
3. It is all a con job with the biggest thieves in the world
4 credit companies = any institution that lends a substantial amount of money

...

When you buy a house lets say 400,000.oo the credit companies finance it for you
Knowing full well you have 75% chance you may never pay it back with interest
So you have a loan 400,000.oo plus lets say 200,000.oo in interest over 30 yrs
So you owe 600,000.oo so they take out insurance in it then sell it off to other creditors
Or at best it is broken into 2 to 3 pieces and sold off with interest kind of pyramid selling
So your 600,000.oo house loan get sold for lets say 700,000.oo
So your credit company made 100,000.oo profit over night buy selling it off as a whole or in bits

...

Then the process starts all over again by who ever brought it so they insure it and sell it of
And the process goes on and on but the best part is after 30 years you actually to pay it off
Your 600,000.oo payments you made on your 400,000.oo house was sold in reality over 1 million dollars
There is infact no way your lender could ever go bust unless they in tern brought up unsecured loans

Its infact it's a type of pyramid selling they the governments tell us not to do but they do it

Banks, credit companies, big business, governments, local councils, and insurance companies all do it

They all try and invest to get rich over night but who actually in reality owns you loan no one can say

...

Its a paper trail that if anyone when looking could be looking for the next 20 yrs or more

You get a letter stating you own it of your original creditor but in reality they sold it off 30 yrs ago

But if the government went looking hard enough they might find they own a share in it along with others

So a house in Australia could very well be owed by people and companies in Europe, America, Asia,

A house in America could very well be owed by people and companies in Russia, Australia, Asia, and Italy

So in reality just how many times has your house or business been brought and sold before you paid it off

You paid for it put when companies go bust in a recession who is the final owner to your property

...

Just who is the final owner to your property the creditor you got it from or the ones that brought of them

Or is it the ones that brought it off them, but who actually has the rights to the title deed in the end

Either way your house or business was paid for many times over before you finally get the deeds in your name

Either way it's a paper trail made to hide the greed and corruption..

That the little people are not aloud to know for we are insignificant in world of business corruption

"UNORTHODOX - CONTROVERSIAL - UNCONVENTIONAL"

Plainly it's called skimming of the top of the profits by governments and businesses alike

GARRY GOSNEY

Just What Are We Looking For

Things we do in order to try and please someone
But what really is the point or if there ever was one
Do we do it to get approval from someone we about
Do we do it to get reassurance that everything is ok?
Or is it to get a parents love and understanding

...

Just why is it that we try to please them
What is it we are really looking for do we ready know?
Is it the thought of knowing we tried our best?
The best son or daughter, the best parent we could be
The best at what, why is it so important to be the best

...

The best we can be at what we do is all we can ask of ourselves
We aim to do the best we can at what ever we choose in life
Win or fail we try our best to be the best we can be
But for what purpose to please the boss, ourselves or someone else
Just what are we looking for out of life and what is it

...

Are we looking for a roll model or someone to look up too?
Are we putting someone on a pedestal that can never be reached?
Just what are we looking for from life
Better yet what are we trying to achieve and why

"UNORTHODOX - CONTROVERSIAL - UNCONVENTIONAL"

17th November The Day I Died

17th November 2008 a day to remember
The day that a son died as far as family goes
The day a son lost all respect and died inside
The day a son lost what he wanted most of all
That day that a mother lost all respect from a son

...

Details of a mother and a son and a stepfather
A stepfather I might add who is not fit to tie dad's shoes
Never alone try to advice or dictate to someone he knows nothing about
It was the worst day in mom's life when she married it
It because its not worthy of its name or the respect of any human

...

It acts like a spoiled baby and will do anything to come between mother and son
It follows mom around like a lap dog whenever I go see mom
Today it said it was going to ring the police and charge me with trespassing
Like I said anything to stop a mother's son from seeing his own birth mother
He is a joke to society his face goes red and his lips go blubber when he's angry

...

In reality he thinks he's a big man because he has a gun but in reality he's small
Small minded, small in stature, and have no commonsense at all and ignorant

GARRY GOSNEY

Never thought I would ever see the day that I would come across someone so ignorant

But guess what I have seen smart sheep and horses than he will ever be in 6 lifetimes

There is not much anyone can really say about someone coming between a parent and a child

...

What can you say about someone coming between a parent and a child regardless of age?

No one has the right to come between parents and child no matter what the circumstances are

There is no age barrier 2 or 170 it is totally irrelevant when stepparents interfere

They interfere in family matters because they are small minded and are the scum of society

They add new meaning to small minded and not worthy of its name or the respect of any human

...

No-one will ever come between me and my kids and they all know it and I mean no-one will

"UNORTHODOX - CONTROVERSIAL - UNCONVENTIONAL"

The Rules of Choice

The choices we make in life
Some say we choose our own parents
But do we really have choices in
Some say our destiny is mapped out at birth

...

Is it destiny or is it society that decides
Is it education or lack of that plays a part
Is it the luck of the draw that wins?
Or is it knowing when to fold and move on

...

Is there any such thing as playing it safe?
If so what does it really mean to play it safe
We have peer pressure but peer pressure is our doing
We put pressure on ourselves to perform for what

...

Society labels every one of us who will succeed or fail
The choices in life are they really ours to decide
We go to work and give it our all only to be told you're fired
But we gave it our all but our best was not good enough

...

We try to please where we can why I never can fully understand
Some say our destiny is mapped out at birth but is it
Parents, schools, work, governments, society all dictate by rules
By rules and regulations all through our life there are rules etc

...

GARRY GOSNEY

Do we have a say in these rules or are they our destiny too
Society said jump so we must jump but why just who makes the rules
Are we living up to someone else's expectations what life should be?
As a child we learn right from wrong but as an adult rules change
...
As an adult rules change to suite their need at any moment in time
When the need arises the rules change so can ones destiny
So what choices do we really have when the rules of choice change?
The rules of choice, the rules of ones destiny mapped out at birth

"UNORTHODOX - CONTROVERSIAL - UNCONVENTIONAL"

He Cries Not for Himself

He is dead inside never to feel again
He cries a thousand tears for what
For what should have been a joyful time
But he cries not for himself but for her

...

He did everything she asked of him
He tried his best at everything that was asked
Deep down inside he knew he wasn't good enough
He know there was no way out but to die inside

...

Will he ever be good enough for her?
That is million-dollar question with only 1 answer
Not in this lifetime nor in the next either
Deep down inside he knew he could never win

...

The odd where never stacked in his favor
There was never an option the deck was pre-stacked
He read the deck all to well for he knew the out come
But he wanted to believed that miracles can happen

...

He was never perfect and never wanted or tried to be
He was no saint that was for sure he didn't want to be
He saw more in the world then he ever wanted to see
But nothing could prepare him of the feeling of death inside

...

GARRY GOSNEY

He is dead inside never to feel again but lives to exist
He cries a thousand tears for what he can never feel again
For what should have been a joyful time but ended in death
He cries not for himself but for her because he's dead inside

"UNORTHODOX - CONTROVERSIAL - UNCONVENTIONAL"

Every Reason Escapes ME

Trying to get in the festive mood
Finding hard to concentrate on anything
Just trying to think of a reason to enjoy
Any reason at all will do but I can't

...

Every reason I had before has escaped me
No children to share the festive mood with
No family to get into the festive mood for
Any reason at all will do but they escape me

...

Finding it hard to concentrate on anything
Every reason I had before has escaped me
Every existence for living is just a memory
Just trying to think of a reason to enjoy

...

Every reason escapes me

GARRY GOSNEY

Let My Heart Whisper

Whispering I love you's
Blowing sweet nothings in your ear
Whispering the things you want to hear
Holding hand in hand as we walk
Watching the stars dance across the sky
Watch lightning dance between the stars
...
Whispering sweet nothings in your ear
Sitting by the lake watching the moon glow
Thinking of all the things I want to say
Thinking of all the good times we shared
Watching the moonbeams glitter on the lake
Watching the stars dance in the moonlight
...
Whispering I love you
Blowing sweet nothings in your ear
Whispering the things you want to hear
Looking into your eyes and seeing you smile
Thinking of all the things I want to say
Wanting to let my heart whisper I love you
...
Let my heart whisper the words I want to hear
Let my heart whisper the words I want to hear

"UNORTHODOX - CONTROVERSIAL - UNCONVENTIONAL"

Many Faces of Christmas

Today I turned TV 23 Nov and watched a movie called
"A man who saved Christmas" about the war and toys
It made me realize that as an adult we face many challenges
But as a child we face the most important challenge of all

The challenge to growing up to have children's dream and wishes
To play childhood games and make children memories
Play, laugh, cry, dreams things that make children grow up
Skip a rope, dolls, meccano sets, toys of all kinds

...

Times of war played out in a boardroom meeting by adults
Adults that lost their dreams of a child growing up
Adults that take a child and turn them into men before there time
Asking families to give up everything even loved ones at Christmas time

...

Christmas is not for adults any more it's just a holiday for most
But for children its memory in the making something they can remember
A lot is asked of families these days with wars and recession taking over
But the most important thing to remember is Christmas time for everyone

...

GARRY GOSNEY

It made me realize that as an adult we face many challenges in life
But the biggest of all is the many faces of Christmas
Remembering all the childhood Christmas's we had together with family
Things that change the world for ever doesn't have to change Christmas

...

Christmas is all about family values and childhood memories
About the birth of Christ and the values of life something to cherish
Christmas is about adults remembering their own childhood Christmas's
About remembering and sharing memories and the values of Christmas

...

Just how many faces of Christmas are there?

"UNORTHODOX - CONTROVERSIAL - UNCONVENTIONAL"

Small Town Christmas

Small town Christmas parade
Floats of all shapes and sizes
Christmas decorations hanging across Main Street
Christmas tree in lights light up the main square
...
Christmas decorations in the shop windows
Christmas songs playing over the loud speakers
Snow flakes falling gently to the ground
Trees covered in Christmas snow and ice.
...
Reindeer dancing and prancing in the snow
Children's laughter heard all over town
Children making snow angels and snowman
The joys of Christmas spirit for young and old
...
Small town Christmas parade
Floats of all shapes and sizes
Everyone dressing up for the holidays
A special time of year for all to share
...
Small town Christmas the best of all

GARRY GOSNEY

Do You Believe

Do you believe in the fantasies of life?
Do you believe in fairytales?
Do you believe in miracles?
Do you believe in Christmas?
The question should be do you want to believe

...

Do you believe in fairytales?
Stories that legions are made of
Fairies flying in and out the garden
Playing games only children can see
Playing for those that truly believe

...

Do you believe in miracles?
Stories that legions are made of
Miracles that come to life when needed
The miracles of birth the growth of life
The miracles in believing anything is possible

...

Do you believe in Christmas?
Stories that legions are made of
The birth of baby Jesus in a manger
Shining stars lighting the way for everyone
Giving us both Enchantment and enlightenment

...

"UNORTHODOX - CONTROVERSIAL - UNCONVENTIONAL"

Do you believe in fairytales?
Do you believe in miracles?
Do you believe in Christmas?
Do you believe in the imagination of life?
But most of all do you believe in you
...
Do you believe?

GARRY GOSNEY

Fake Promises and Broken Truths

Is there a real estate agent that does not lie?
The answer to that is no in every sense of the word
They try everything to avoid their responsibilities
They are high on promise but every promise is fake

...

When you sell a place with them they promise the moon
But in promising the moon they over charge you for it
High fees for a photo in the paper and their window
Just having it on their books cost 10s of thousands

...

10s of thousands dollars for what 1 paper add and a photo
50 houses on the books at 20 percent fees adds up
To 100s of thousands dollars per mth if they are good at it
But they don't go out of their way to sell it you need to walk in

...

House rental properties is a joke they do very little
Unit rentals not much better but they still over charge
Strata managers well that's the best one of all of them
They jump up and down at you telling you what to do

...

But they themselves do apparently nothing but take money
They rip the owners off they don't care how the place looks
They employ a caretaker but give them nothing to work with
They send you to get quotes for what you need but why

...

"UNORTHODOX - CONTROVERSIAL - UNCONVENTIONAL"

But why you may ask its so they can be made to feel good
Made to feel like they are actually doing something
But in fact they're not doing a thing and it's to shut you up
It makes them look good to the owners wherever they live

...

In the mean time nothing gets done through buck passing
Buck passing and fake promises and lies and broken truths
Just what part of the real estate agents do at the finest
In the mean time the tenants live in squalor

...

In squalor while real estate agents neglect their responsibilities
They tell the tenants that they must be responsible
Yet they shed all responsibility for their actions and buck pass
Yet they jump up and down at you telling you what to do

...

GARRY GOSNEY

Real-Estate Agents in the Mid-West Geraldton

West Australia mid west region has the worst estate agents around
Lets start with 1st National they are the easiest one to start with
First they promise to do repairs but don't they blame the owners
They use every trick in the book to shed their responsibilities
After 3 mths of asking politely and getting no where
Then you threaten to take them to court but they try to call your bluff
Knowing full well that you have photos to back everything up
All documented evidence to take then court to get a doorknob but on
Then they evict you when your lease is up for renewal and say it's your fault
They are truly a slumlord with no respect for tenants or owners property

...

Then you have the professional's strata managers who use every trick in the book
Every trick in the book not to give you proper power and gas bills
All so they can skim off the top of the bills by adding 10 or 20 dollars to it
And still don't do any maintenance either but charge tenants plenty for it
They are truly a slumlord with no respect for tenants or owners property

...

Then you have KALAZICH SMITH who has no respect for tenants or owners
As landlords they are on a scale of 1 to 10 .. 1 being crap 10 being great

"UNORTHODOX - CONTROVERSIAL - UNCONVENTIONAL"

They are a 2 it's the best rating anyone could ever give them

As a strata managers on a scale of 1 to 10 .. 1 being crap 10 being great

They are on the same scale as 1st national and professional realty is a -1

They are all minus 1 as they lie through there teeth and shed responsibility

They shed responsibility and buck pass but are all talk and no action

High on promise to do things, blow sunshine where the sun don't shine but do nothing

...

They are a disgrace to there profession and how they stay in business no one knows

They show no respect for the owners of rental units and even less for tenants

They abuse their rights to by stand over tactics that is if you let them

They abuse the powers the owners give them and entrust them with

They break every law known to man when it comes to tenants rights (photos taken)

All documents and photos can be produced in court if need be

They all expect good tenants to live in squalor because they don't want to do maintenance

...

With the recession setting in we can all hope they close there doors for good

GARRY GOSNEY

They Deserve Life Death by Natural Causes

I have to laugh at the West Australian Government
It so idiotic you cannot help but laugh at it if you didn't you would cry
"Opposition legal affairs spokesman Jim McGinty proposed amendments saying
the legislation failed to ensure suitable penalties for serious crimes "
Is a true idiot when he was police minister and attorney general?
He did nothing at all but boast about how good he was at his job
and pass the buck and neglected all his responsibilities to the public
..
He alone made West Australia the laughing stock of the world
Him and the carpenter government of 2007 made it a criminal heaven for all
If you're white and get charged with gangland bashings they get full penalty
Full penalty for murder is 21 yrs life .. or 20 for attempted murder
if aboriginal male or female they slap on the wrist and don't do it again
But they have been given a license to kill or maim, as the law does nothing
..
On Tuesday 3 dec 08, Mathew Roy McDonald, 22, was jailed for five years for
the manslaughter of William (Bill) John Rowe who was murdered on Christmas
Day, but he may serve less than three years before becoming eligible for parole.

"UNORTHODOX - CONTROVERSIAL - UNCONVENTIONAL"

Mr Rowe, 49, died after being struck on the side of the head with the cricket bat while he was with family at the Sunset Beach car park in Geraldton, in the state's midwest, on Christmas night dec 07.

He was in a life coma with the prospect of a life on life support

a living vegetable with no prospect of ever coming out the coma

Life support was switched off 26 december 2007 by his family

a day that they will never forget, a day the family will take to their grave

..

The Geraldton police downgraded the murder charge to manslaughter

a gang of 20+ aboriginals that all assaulted and murdered him and his family

Ranging from 12 yrs old to 40 yrs old all assaulted the Rowe family

and then the judge did the highest insult of all gave him a plea bargain

when every one of them should have been given the death penalty

The death penalty or the equivalent in life behind bars no parole forever

..

It is a disgrace when aboriginals get a slap on the wrist for gang murders

and the government let them get away with it and condone it by doing nothing

There are 5 laws in Australia and they do not meet in the middle

Politicians well they make the laws to suite themselves when ever needed

Police corruption all they get is slap on the wrist and a posting change

GARRY GOSNEY

Magistrates are untouchable and blame everyone else for there corruption

Aboriginals well the government pussyfoots around them and turn a blind eye

Whites well they get the book thrown at them too the full extent of the law

...

When what should be done is put them all in prison for life or death by nature

Life death by natural causes and everyone treated evenly gang bashing get life

Regardless whether white indigenous or aboriginal indigenous Australia

Immigrants anyone for that matter living in Australia permanent or visiting

gang bashing are bashings by the scum of the earth and has no nationality

it has no nationality, race, greed or colour so it leaves no choice life

they should never be given a choice, they gave no choice to the life they took

eye for an eye, life for a life, live by the sword you shall die by the sword

..

the bible saids ..

let no man take a life unless he is prepared to have his life taken

"UNORTHODOX - CONTROVERSIAL - UNCONVENTIONAL"

God Show Us the Way Home

God the times are harder now because of the recession
People loosing their jobs because of hard time
Yes God it is a man made recession brought on by greed
We have people away and dying trying to fight wars
Trying to fight a war on terrorism and war on greed
...
Yes God we deserve everything we get
Yes God we are our own worst enemy
Yes God we don't deserve your pity or help
Yes God we are a disgrace we have lost all life values
Yes God we should all be ashamed of the way we behave
...
God give us the power to learn from our mistakes
God I can't give you one good reason at all to help us
But God we are your children so we are always told
But as children God we all make plenty of mistakes
God in away we are asking if you will walk with us
...
Walk with us in our time of need at this special time
Christmas will extra hard for many in the years ahead
The days will be even harder as time get tougher
God walk with us and show us the light and a way out
God give us the strength to go forward with our heads high
...

GARRY GOSNEY

Please look after our friends and family in time of war
Please look after all the unknown soldiers, victims of war
Please show them that all is not lost, we will survive
Christmas time is a time of hope, faith, love and charity
God walk with us this Christmas and show us they way home
...
God walk with us and show us the lesson we need to learn
God show us the way home

"UNORTHODOX - CONTROVERSIAL - UNCONVENTIONAL"

Christmas And Feeling Special

Mistletoe and bright coloured lights
Warm fire and telling stories of yesterday
Sipping warm chocolate and looking outside
Watching snowflakes gently flutter down
...

Singing Christmas carols in a street parade
Looking at decorations in the store fronts
Driving down main street looking at the decoration
Or just watching snowfall gently on the trees
...

Christmas time is near
Christmas laughter is in the wind
Christmas is waking up to presents
Christmas is waking up and feeling special
...

Christmas time is sharing a smile, a hug with friends
Christmas time is wishing a stranger happy Christmas
Christmas time is time to believe in the unknown
Christmas time is a time for rejoicing for young, old
...

Mistletoe and bright coloured lights
Singing Christmas carols in a street parade
Christmas is waking up and feeling special
Christmas time is a time for rejoicing for young, old
...

GARRY GOSNEY

Merry Christmas everyone for you made me feel special
Merry Christmas everyone for everyone is special to me
Christmas and feeling special

"UNORTHODOX - CONTROVERSIAL - UNCONVENTIONAL"

The Meaning of a Handshake

A handshake just what does it mean can be a lot or nothing
Really for a first time meeting it's fake
Fake because it is only out of common courtesy
There is no respect or anything else in at all
How can you respect someone you have never met before?

...

A handshake of friendship is a handshake earned
A handshake of respect is a handshake earned
Both are earned over a period of time mostly years
Both are earned by honesty and trust in each other
Trust in knowing you are not being lied to or use

...

I was always told never trust anyone who laughs a lot
Who tries to blow sunshine where the sun don't shine
Who cannot look you straight in the eye every time?
Who always promise things and never delivers on them
A handshake with these people is as fake as they are

...

In my 50+ yrs I have found the most honest handshake
The most honest handshakes come from the poor
They have nothing to loose but their dignity
Something I find rich people know nothing about
Rich people walk over everyone and abuse everyone they meet

...

GARRY GOSNEY

They respect no one without money or the same as them
What they never realize though their own ignorance
Their own ignorance is that the poor don't care what they have
The poor don't care about their money or their fancy cars
All the poor want respect for the work they do for the rich

...

You think respect is a strong word then show them courtesy
Like you would a dog or a cat they don't care if you're rich
We the poor don't care either way how you got it or kill for it
A poor mans handshake is 80% based on their word, there bond
A rich mans handshake is 90% based on lies and false promises

...

A rich person tries to buy what they cannot get .. Respect ..
Respect why because they do not know how to give it or its meaning
They think everyone has a price yes I do and you can not afford it
My handshake of friendship is earned and not for sale
My handshake of respect is earned and not for sale
My handshake of trust, friendship, respect, dignity is not for sale

...

Very few will ever or ever has been able to afford my price
My handshakes will never be walked on and will never be abused
How far will you go to buy respect and keep your own self-respect?
How much are you willing to sell your dignity and respect for
I can assure you of one thing I will never be brought or sold

...

What I give I give freely and only when I choose to do so freely

"UNORTHODOX - CONTROVERSIAL - UNCONVENTIONAL"
Believe The Magic of Christmas

Merry Christmas everyone young and old
Snowflakes gently flowing in the wind
Ground covered in layers of snowflakes
The wind whistling through trees

...

Christmas time a favorite time of year
Listening to carols in the domain on TV
Singing along with all the favorite songs
Just closing your eyes and picturing mood

...

Picturing the essential part of Christmas
A baby was born in a manger for all mankind
Picturing the sounds and joys of Christmas
Snowflakes falling gently in the breeze

...

Just close your eyes and picture mood
Picture the essential part of Christmas
A baby was born for all mankind to believe in
Christmas time a favorite time of year

...

Merry Christmas everyone young and old
Believe in the unknown, believe in the faith
Believe in the magic of the Christmas spirit
Believe in the magic of the Christmas spirit

GARRY GOSNEY
Revitalization of Life Memories

Two things in life we are sure of birth and death
Years 1 to 5 the innocent years in the life cycle
The fragile years of life the learning years of life
The first words, fist stand, first fall, first walk
The first run, the first cry the first laugh
Then you have fun years 5 to 16 first day at school
The first day at high school and the pass out parade
Then you have the teens full of mixed emotions
Then there are 20 to 35 the indestructible years of
Football, tennis, bungy jumping, sky diving etc etc
Broken bones etc but they will do it all over again
Then there is the overlap years 25 to 50 work, work
Must build a life and have a family and settle down
Then there is what's called the twilight years 50 to 65
The dreaming stage of what is ahead in retirement
The reflection stage over what kinder life have I lead
Then there is the old age stage 65 and above reflecting
Oh what a life, if only, what could have been?
The fragile years of life the learning years of life
Learning we are not as young as we use to be
In away learning all the things we have forgotten
Learning to walk slower and learning how to young again
Learning how to young again at an old age is not the end
It can be the new beginning to an old lifestyle
Revitalization = bringing again into activity and prominence
Grandchildren and great grandchildren bring joy to everyone

"UNORTHODOX - CONTROVERSIAL - UNCONVENTIONAL"

Grand parents can bring joy and understanding to everyone
They also bring a lifetime of education to the young
But all the time life is educating them as they grow
The education school of hard knocks the best school of all
But the hardest knock of all is loosing a loved one
But one thing I have learnt is that the memories seam to grow
Why I have never been able to find out but to me I know its true
Revitalization of life into activity and prominence memories
Never let go of the memories of loved ones gone
They have moved on but the memories will ever last
Young and old they all live and share memories of love ones past
I call it revitalization of life memories

GARRY GOSNEY
Just How Honest Will He Be

One man stands alone and walks a rough road
With the weight of the world on his shoulders
Just how honest will this man be?
Will he right the wrongs done by the previous government?
Or will he condone the corruption within its ranks
Just how honest will this man be?

...

One man stands alone amongst uncharted waters
Just how honest will this man be?
The world has change and we have changed with it
Is it for the better or for the worst time will tell
They say move over let the man walk the talk give him ago
He walks uncharted waters in a changed world

...

One man stood alone on a hill and gave a sermon he was God
Now another man stands alone on a hill, capital hill
But with a different kind of sermon in mind his name OBAMA
The times are hard and the times need change he said
Change from big business greed, and corruption
Change from government lies, corruption and deceit

...

"UNORTHODOX - CONTROVERSIAL - UNCONVENTIONAL"

One man alone trying to make his action accountable
Trying to make the governments of the world accountable
Just how honest will this man be in a world of corruption?
One man stands alone and walks a rough road
One man stands alone amongst uncharted waters
One man stands alone on a hill, capital hill, President Obama

...

Just how honest will this man be?
Will he right the wrongs done to people who visit is country?
Will he help the victims of an unjust corrupt system?
Will he right the wrongs or will he condone them
Just how honest will this man be that walks alone?
One man stands alone and just how honest will he be

...

Just how honest will this man be?

GARRY GOSNEY

Raging Out Of Control

Fire, fire, fire raging out of control
Up gullies and down mountains
Counting houses one two three
Counting cars one two three

...

Complete farms being consumed
Livestock, wildlife everything gone
Sheds, houses, history everything gone
Like there was no tomorrow

...

Black smoke as far as the eye can see
The sounds of people screaming
The sound of the roar of the fire
A horrific feeling to say the least

...

People running blindly in all directions
Everyone trying to selvage what they can
Everyone looking out for each other
Will they survive or will they perish

...

People trying escape in all direction
No warning sirens in place at all
Everyone left to their own devices
Should I leave or should I stay

...

"UNORTHODOX - CONTROVERSIAL - UNCONVENTIONAL"

Thousands of questions need to be answered
How, when and why did the fires happen
Could it have been stopped?
So many lives lost and more to come

...

Some have complete families wipeout
Some have friends and loved ones wipeout
Town nearly wiped off the map, as we know it
Just when and how will it all end

...

Fire fire fire raging out of control
Counting houses one two three
Counting cars one two three
Counting lives twenty, thirty, hundred at a time

...

The worst destruction in the history of Australia

GARRY GOSNEY

In Our Time of Need

Prayers both answered and unanswered
Prayers God help us in our time of need
Help us all to survive this fiery inferno
Help us to understand why us what did we do
Why did the fiery gates of hell to open up?
...
God help us to survive this fiery inferno
Teach us how, when and where we went wrong
Help find who started the inferno
Help use get the answers we seek
God help us to understand as a nation
...
God why did our prayers go unanswered
Families destroyed and friends lost
Homes and towns wiped of the map
Children of all ages seeing death
Why God why was we saved and others die
...
God give us the strength to rebuild
To rebuild our hearts and friendships
To rebuild our towns and homes
To rebuild a nation to its finest
To extend a hand when ever it is needed
...

"UNORTHODOX - CONTROVERSIAL - UNCONVENTIONAL"

God please show us our failures
God give us the strength to learn from them
God teach us what it is you want us to know
Thank you for uniting a nation in our time of need
Thank you for showing us that we are not alone

...

GARRY GOSNEY

The Basics of Life in a Recession

Times have changed in away never seen before
Jobs being lost in the thousands daily
Homes being repossess in the tens of thousands
Everyone wondering why me why is this happening

..

Ten years in the making all the signs was there
Yet people still persist they had no idea
It makes one wonder why we have TV, radio and newspapers
For it looks as no one actually reads them any more

..

The comics are great in the newspapers and magazines
The music is about the only thing everyone listens too
Talk show hosts only interested in the area they live in
Its as though people don't care anymore about the big picture

..

Just what will it take to wake them up to all there bad habits
Everything one does has a change reaction that affects someone
It's the greed of the oil companies that started this recession
It's the greed of the governments that fueled big business greed

..

Only when their corner of the world is affected
They start to think by that time its to late
Then they start on the oh pitiful me why me
They only answer is they have never been made accountable

..

"UNORTHODOX - CONTROVERSIAL - UNCONVENTIONAL"

Over priced food and clothing that no one can afford or sustain
Over price cars and homes that no one can afford or sustain
Easy access to credit with no control by anyone at all
Company executives and owners getting million dollar payoffs
..
Everything in the days of our lives is getting out of reach
Everything is getting out of our means to pay for them
80 percent living on a day by day by credit card to credit card
Everyone has forgotten what the basics are to life and how to live
..
We have forgotten what the basics of life are
In order to with stand and survive the recession
We need to get back to the basics of life and what life means
God show us the way back to the basics of life

GARRY GOSNEY

I Call It Gods Plan for the Future

The world as we know it to be has gone
The harsh reality is the fact it's not the same
It will never be anymore there is no number 1
There is no number 2 to fall back on anymore
Each country can only rely on themselves from now on
The export and import giants have become unreliable

...

The major countries that dictated to the world
Well they can dictate no more for their words are useless
Useless words that bankrupted a country throughout lies and deceit
That bankrupted the world through lies and greed for the best part
Political leaders that turned a blind eye to the corruption
Yet they had both there hands out for pay offs under the table

...

Tent cities and shantytowns popping wherever there is vacant land
The poorest of the poor countries living in tents and shanties
Now the poor of the richest countries forced to live the same way
It is both funny and sad and ironic to see them in tents and shanties
But at the same time it is making the poor richer and the rich poorer
The poor are richer then ever before because they know how to survive

...

The middle class and the rich are poorer as they have more to loose
They live well outside their means they all need to have the best of things
Everything new everything must be better than the neighbours up the street

"UNORTHODOX - CONTROVERSIAL - UNCONVENTIONAL"

Take-aways and fancy cars to designer ware the best life has to offer
But what they forgot about was how to live life the simple way
Life is like throwing a ball what goes up must come down
...
Prices go up and must come down life can only sustain a high for so long
Then life will deal a low that can last just as long as the high
It teaches us where we went wrong as a society and why it happened
It gives us a 5 yr. cooling of period where nothing goes up or down
It gives a chance to set things in motion that normally would not be looked at
A different way of thinking about things for the future
...
I would like to call its Gods plan for the future

GARRY GOSNEY
A Publishers Dream an Authors Nightmare

Delights in the world of big business world
It is full of corruption lies and deceit
The moment you expose their weakness they lie more
They can never take the blame for their own uselessness

..

That would mean that they are no longer in charge
They can no longer dictate the terms of agreement
So they terminate your terms of agreement by blaming you
When all you were trying to do was expose there own stupidity

..

Stupidity in they way they conduct their business practices
But the best part is their total contempt for their clients
They are ignorant to their prospective clients needs and wishes
They actually think they Gods gift and the answer to everything

..

Reality check they are arrogant, ignorant, and full of lies and deceit
But because they are publishers you must beg and go yes sir everytime
Reality check guys no we don't have to but up with your abuse anymore
Reality check your greed, lies and deceit will now be exposed

..

You're in a profession that should get things right the first time
Not take 2 or 3 goes to get it right and charge more for your stuff ups
Publishers all over the world should know how to copy things the 1st time
But I have yet to find a publisher that can get it right the first time

..

But they always say it's your fault that's the way you sent it what a joke

They don't realize that we have the originals at home and send them copies

The reason we do that is because he have to show them up to their own mistakes

Yet they still try and but the blame back on to you for their mistakes

..

The publishing industry is full of lies, deceit and uselessness in its ranks

They always try every trick in the book to extort more money than what its worth

They come up with every excuse under the sun and even try to make up new ones

But one thing they can never cover up is their incompetence, lies and deceit

..

A publishers dream and an author's nightmare

GARRY GOSNEY

Failure In the Family Department

What is happing to her family?
Just what is happening around her?
Her world is falling apart big time
She has questions but no answers

..

Her children fighting amongst themselves
Each one ringing the police on the other
Each one not communicating to the others
Each one talking legal action on the other

..

Brother against sister, sister against brother
Just how, when and why did her world fall apart
Could it have been stopped if she was there?
Just how can she save the family she loves?

..

God give her the strength to try to understand
To understand the reasons behind it all
To try and find a solution to the problem
Better yet can there be a solution or an answer

..

God just what will it take to heal the wounds
God better yet can the wounds ever be healed
God give her the encouragement she needs
She needs to move forward and find the answers

..

"UNORTHODOX - CONTROVERSIAL - UNCONVENTIONAL"

Is she doing the right thing in loving her family?
Is she doing the right thing in splitting up a family?
Separating brother and sister and brother and brother
Just what will the out come be for better or worse
..
God I pray that you and help us find a answer
I pray she will find the answer she seeks
I pray that she will find the love she's looking for
God it's been along time coming please guide us god
..
Family problems but is there a family solution
Can answers be found so that unity can be restored?
God just where did I go wrong in family values
God why do I feel like a failure in the family department

GARRY GOSNEY

Sometimes Things Are Better Left Unsaid

I have learnt sometimes things are better left unsaid
I have learnt never to talk about my past to anyone
The ones you think you can trust are the ones you can't
For they are the ones that throw it back at ya every time

...

They throw failed marriages at ya and say they know why
They throw failed fatherhood at ya and they know why
They blame you for everything that happened to them
They say you should have known better it's your country

...

They tell your children not to come over nothing here for them
They say they know why your children don't come to visit
They say you're an abusive man because you swear and are loud
Yes I do and am it is something I have done all my life

...

Right or wrong as it maybe is something I have to live with
Words are the hardest thing for me to find and have been all my life
Yes and they will continue to be until I die (I am dyslexic)
Words I should use I can't always find so I swear out frustration

...

Frustration that I should know better for I should know the words
Frustration that I can't say the exact words I want to say when I need to
I know what I want to say but it doesn't always come out the way it should
Yes I have written books but it don't make it any easier to speak the works

"UNORTHODOX - CONTROVERSIAL - UNCONVENTIONAL"

...

People that should understand you don't and that hurts the most of all

They throw your past failures right back at ya so you relive them over and over

Saying you will never be anything without them but you feel like nothing with them

So you go into a hibernation mode only coming out when you think it's safe

...

Just when will I learn the past / present and future don't mix

You tell someone your past only to find out you relive it in the present

You live the present only to be reminded of it all in the future

Right or wrong no one needs to be reminded of their past failures

...

Am I proud of my life and the way it's gone answer YES and NO

Any regrets answer YES and NO

Would I do the same all over again PROBERLY?

Sometimes things are better left unsaid

GARRY GOSNEY

What Do You Want from Me

What do I want from you? The answer is nothing but friendship

What do I need from you? The answer nothing but friendship

Why did you marry me? The answer is try to give you something better

Nothing perfect but hopefully something better than you have had in the past

...

I'm not interested in your past as it's your past

I'm interested in only the present as it is now

I'm not interested in the future as no one knows what it will bring

My only interest is trying to achieve a dream and make it come true

...

We can plan for the future but the outcome is not in our control

God controls the future we can only hope our future works out

We live our life to the fullest we can for we try to live our dreams

Our dreams, wishes, hopes all rolled into the past / present / future

...

Past as a driving force, present as a way of planning for the future

Not everything goes according to plan A but there is always plan B

What do you want from me, answer nothing but friendship

Friendship just two people going in the same parallel direction

...

"UNORTHODOX - CONTROVERSIAL - UNCONVENTIONAL"

Will it be on a destructive path who knows as the present is destructive?

A fork in the road do we both go right or left or go separate ways

Will we part as friends or will we be enemies that the question

What am I looking for answer nothing but friendship along the way?

...

What do you want from me

GARRY GOSNEY

Ultimatum

To give someone the ultimatum is not the best thing to do

You may find the answers not to your liking but you asked for it

You can't change people or cultures but you can try to understand them

Different countries, different customs, different ways of doing things

You can't change the way people talk or the way they act

By putting words into their mouth telling them what to say and how to say it

Ultimatum = love me this way or not at all

7 out of 10 will go not at all

Ultimatum = you could have said this !!!! Instead of that

7 out of 10 will say I could have said a lot of things but didn't

I can only talk the way I know how it may not be the best but it's me

You can only talk the way you know how but that is you

Ultimatum = if you can't make love to me this way then don't

7 out of 10 will opt for don't

I can love you the only way I know how my way

You can only love me the only way you know how your way

Ultimatum = talk to me this way or not at all

Some talk quietly some are loud when they talk but it's their normal way

But it does not mean that they don't care about you it's just there way

But fingers in your ears and going naa naa naa does not help the communication

"UNORTHODOX - CONTROVERSIAL - UNCONVENTIONAL"

It fact it helps to turn them off complete from any form of communication

It just goes to show your wasting your time the ultimatum = is to forget it

I can't change you for you are woman, you can't change me for I am man

We can accept each other for whom and what they are and try to understand them

That is the best anyone can do is try to understand the ones they love their way

Love is an ultimatum of give and take, freedom to be one's self in a relationship

Not how you make me look to the world or they way I make the world look at you

It's not about how your family see me or how my family sees you it's about two people

It's about two people going in the same direction on the same road called " LIFE "

It's about two people helping each other to achieve each others goals along the way

It's about two people knowing when to stay on the merry-go-round and when to get off

The ultimatum should I stay or should I go

You may find the answers not to your liking but you asked for it

If my way of loving you is NOT GOOD ENOUGH for you

Then I'm NOT GOOD ENOUGH for you

Then it's time to get off the merry-go-round and move on

For I'm not good enough so I'm getting of because you not good enough FOR ME

That is my Ultimatum

GARRY GOSNEY

Re Your All Your Books

Garry,

What can I possibly say that hasn't been said already- the feelings you are able to so freely put down on paper- wow- its just unreal- to know you or not know you - the intensity of your emotions is so deep and so real- I could feel them - every hurt- every tear- every laugh- and every pain- - believe me it was an exhausting trip- going into your books- this second book is equally as rivetting as the first- and has just as much emotion- I always read from cover to cover- there's no missing bits- and so I sat determined to follow your life through with you- beside you all the way- wanting to hear your heart sing and to be healed - Maybe next book- your will find what you so desperately seek- the love of another human being who can understand you - heal your heart and help you through your life with all your pains and hurts - some one who is balm to your heart- for surely you deserve it my friend -

Caz- an Aussie Friend

"UNORTHODOX - CONTROVERSIAL - UNCONVENTIONAL"

A Letter About the Author's First Book

Hi Garry,

I finally have the chance to share my thoughts on your book – One Aussie Endeavours.
Firstly, thank you for allowing me to read it. Although I haven't yet read it cover to cover, I have read many of the poems and stories within. Each piece feels so different from the one before it.
I feel as though I can sense your mood while reading—whether you're having a good or a bad day. Some poems are incredibly deep, sincere, and true to life. Others make me feel a sense of sadness, as if they were written during darker days—moments that haunt you. And it all comes through so clearly in your work.
If I had to sum it up in a single sentence, it would be this:
"I feel like I'm reading your diary."
Your name may not be mentioned, but the thoughts are so real—both the good and the bad.
The more I read, the more I want to keep reading. I never know what to expect from one title to the next. Some titles give a hint, but it's not until I read them through, top to bottom, that I can fully appreciate the depth and effort you've poured into this great book.
Once again, thank you, Garry, for sharing these intimate moments with all of us. That's how I see this book—it's a collection of your personal reflections: feelings of love, dreams, desire, lust, hate, distrust, trust, loneliness, fulfillment, happiness, and sadness—and so much more.
Not only are the words special, but the pictures are as well. Your travels add something truly unique to this book and set it apart from other poetry books I've read.

Thank you, Garry.
Your friend always,
Kate – Australia

The Unorthodox Poet: Garry Gosney

Garry Gosney writer of One Aussie Endeavours : has surpassed his talents by showing us all what happens when one man persist to develop and improve as he has shown us, with his style of growth and delivered in his knew book titled
MYUNORTHODOX HEARTS Desires Loves Prayers: Lyrics.
Here he has shown us he no longer is just a simple man writing a few poems; he has become a true writer, a published author of now three books with style and a talent uniquely his own.
The UNORTHODOX POET
Please be inspired by seeing the growth off one mans endeavours in the world or writing

Anne

"UNORTHODOX - CONTROVERSIAL - UNCONVENTIONAL"

One Aussies Endeavours Vol 2 Desires Memories Dreams Lyrics

(Unorthodox Australian Poet)
By Garry W Gosney

Book 4- Another brilliant book of poems, odes, lyrics and everyday events as seen through the eyes of Garry, the Unorthodox Australian Poet.
As in his previous books - his emotions are poured into each page, and wether you read from cover to cover, or just individual poems, you can't help but feel the raw emotions which come from himself. Considering his Dyslexic condition, together with his diabetes, ADD, ADHD,
and other serious health problems - his writing never mentions his own pains and hardships. He never fails to think of his fellow humans and write what he sees and feels within. His topics cover things such as pure love, the surroundings from which his ideas come from, his emotion as at the time of writing, the news topics and events of the day, a scene from the street or his mind or anything that comes to light. Things that reach news headlines, are often the next topic in the next poem. – to him writing is relaxation, despite doing half a dozen things at a time eg: like he watches tv, dj's in a chat room, has the music going on his computer and is writing his next poem, he calls it writting by distraction the only way he knows how something we all take for granted. something as simple as a single word can trigger his next idea for a poem. Having read most of his books I have seen the tremendous improvement in each successive book.
Good Luck my friend

Caz Brown– West Aus.

From: Max101st@aol.com

To: Perth_Desperado – Garry Gosney

Subject: Web Page

Date: Sun, 29 Jul 2001 14:03:34 EDT

Garry,

Your web page is very well done; I enjoyed reading it very much.

My name is Ted McCormick, and I live with my wife in Flint, Michigan, USA. I am the editor of *MixedMediaStudios* – http://www.mixedmediastudios.com.

I was surfing the net when I came across your web page. I am a Vietnam veteran and visited your country during my tour of duty in September 1970. I have a section in *MixedMediaStudios* dedicated to the war.

You might be interested in the *Literature* page at MixedMedia. I have all of Jack London's works published, along with a biography of Ernest Hemingway, and many links for artists.

Keep up the excellent work and never become discouraged when you have something to say.

Your Friend,

Ted McCormick

"UNORTHODOX - CONTROVERSIAL - UNCONVENTIONAL"

From: Max101st@aol.com

To: Perth_Desperado – Garry Gosney

Subject: Web Site

Date: Sun, 29 Jul 2001 19:49:32 EDT

Garry,

Excellent job.

I will save your page and publish some of your work in my next edition.

Unfortunately, I just uploaded the current issue last week, so we're looking at next month or possibly later.

It's great to see that some people still care about what America stands for.

I saw on your page that you like German Shepherds—they are my favorite breed also.

My Shepherd, "Jack", passed away last year from cancer of the spleen. That is him on the cover page of *MixedMedia*. I miss him every day. I didn't even know he was sick until the day he passed—he died in my arms.

Keep up the good work, Garry, and stay in touch.

Ted

From: Max101st@aol.com

To: Perth_Desperado – Garry Gosney

Subject: (no subject)

Date: [undated]

Good work, Garry…

I will place your work on this page:

http://www.mixedmediastudios.com/page15.html

Go to the page and check it out.

Great picture of Jack Kerouac—he started the Beatnik craze in the fifties with his book *Route 66* (he looks a little drunk in this shot… LOL). It was a good book, although he never really wrote anything afterward that compared with *66*.

One of my favorite writers was Jack London. His complete works are there: *Call of the Wild, To Build a Fire, John Barleycorn*, etc. It's a must-read—compliments of SCU at Berkeley. He was an amazing writer and lived a life most of us dream about.

I also have a section for Mississippi writers—great stuff. The State of Mississippi has produced some great talent.

And, of course, I've included Ernest Hemingway. I love his books.

Robert Anderson (Little Hawk) is a Korean War veteran and amateur writer who is also a friend I met through the Viet Vet chat site I belong to.

Your poetry will add a nice touch to the page.

I get lost there often myself.

Later,

Ted

"UNORTHODOX - CONTROVERSIAL - UNCONVENTIONAL"

Postscript by Garry Gosney:

Ted McCormick was the English teacher who encouraged me in what I do.

I never did find out what you meant by *writing in 3s*... Seven years on, Ted, and I'm still trying to understand what you meant.

Ted, wherever you and your family are, I hope you're all safe.

GOD BLESS,

Garry

www.ingramcontent.com/pod-product-compliance
Lightning Source LLC
Chambersburg PA
CBHW061219070526
44584CB00029B/3893